It's Delightful! It's Delo

De Soto
AUTOMOBILES

Dennis David

Iconografix

Iconografix
PO Box 446
Hudson, Wisconsin 54016 USA

Library of Congress Control Number: 2006926929

ISBN-13: 978-1-58388-172-9
ISBN-10: 1-58388-172-7

06 07 08 09 10 11 6 5 4 3 2 1

Printed in China

Cover and book design by Dan Perry

Copyedited by Suzie Helberg

On the cover: The Virgil Exner Forward Look styling theme was prominently displayed in DeSoto's advertising for 1956. Two-tone colors were all the rage.

Book Proposals

Iconografix is a publishing company specializing in books for transportation enthusiasts. We publish in a number of different areas, including Automobiles, Auto Racing, Buses, Construction Equipment, Emergency Equipment, Farming Equipment, Railroads & Trucks. The Iconografix imprint is constantly growing and expanding into new subject areas.

Authors, editors, and knowledgeable enthusiasts in the field of transportation history are invited to contact the Editorial Department at Iconografix, Inc., PO Box 446, Hudson, WI 54016.

CONTENTS

ACKNOWLEDGMENTS

When Dylan Frautschi, the Managing Editor from Iconografix Incorporated, and I first started talking about a book on DeSoto, the first step was to see what was already written on the subject. There are certainly very few books written on DeSoto, but most were written while only mentioning DeSoto along with something else. Just as the DeSoto automobile often shared parts with its Dodge, Plymouth, and Chrysler cousins, it is always mentioned in conjunction with these same family members. But here was a chance to let the DeSoto brand have its day in the sun; a book that focuses solely on DeSoto automobiles, and the story it has to tell. This is not a book that defines each and every serial number of every model DeSoto ever built. Quite simply, it's a

book that tells the story of an American car company that gave us some great cars. Indeed DeSoto's history parallels that of the United States of America, for there are generations of Americans who literally grew up with DeSoto. It's a story of the company's history, but it's also a story of passion.

To this end, many fine people contributed historical information for this project, which resulted in what you see before you. I am a writer, but the ensemble that I was able to put together to help with this book made me truly excited about the project. Certainly the Foreword by noted car collector and actor Edward Herrmann makes for a wonderful beginning to this work, and I thank him for that. Also appearing in this book are several previously unpublished works of art by noted artist John Satterthwaite. His amazing ability to capture the incredible style and detail of DeSoto made for a wonderful addition to this book.

This writing would not have happened without the hard work and effort of many people. Photos must be assembled, information must be gathered, and sources must be checked and rechecked for accuracy. In the case of DeSoto, there are a few people that know this material better than anyone, and their editing skills made all the difference. I would like to thank Les Pesavento for many of the photos, factory data, and careful editing of the text. His lifetime career with the Chrysler Corporation and extensive collection of DeSoto automobiles and factory material certainly qualifies him as a leading authority on the subject. I would also like to thank Doug and Chris Dressler, who are not only knowledgeable in DeSoto history, but who also possess an incredible eye for accuracy. Lee Exline, always one to travel the unbeaten path, is also a recognized authority on some of the more obscure aspects of DeSoto, and he contributed greatly to some of the most interesting parts of the DeSoto story; I thank him as well. Thanks also to Eugene Weiss for his first-hand knowledge of DeSoto's history. Award winning automotive journalist Jeff Godshall also clarified several aspects of DeSoto's history, and I thank him for his expert insight.

Of course, the National DeSoto Club, the keeper of the DeSoto torch, made this book better. Lanette Peiffer, Judith Alta Kidder, Dean Mullinax, Roderick Sergiades, and many other members of the club answered my endless questions and assisted whenever possible. Club members Tony and Christine deFoster, Joseph White, Eugene Kidder, Bobbi Youngblood, Doug and Arlene Conran, Wayne Newman, Albert DellaBianca, and Doug Dressler allowed me to photograph their cars, and I thank them for that.

I would also like to thank Mark Patrick from the Detroit Historical Collection, one of the world's greatest treasuries of automotive related data. Of course the fine folks at the AACA Library & Research Center in Hershey, Pennsylvania were of invaluable assistance, as were the Society of Automotive Historians Ralph H. Dunwoodie Automotive Research Archives located there. My good friend Leroy Cole also provided insight, and I would be remiss if I did not mention the help of my good friend, historian and journalist Kit Foster, who was always there with answers whenever I had a question. The research for this book was helped along and analyzed by Dr. Pat Foster of Central Connecticut State University, and noted automotive historian Dr. Paul Sable.

Lastly, my wife Susan is my "first reader" of all of my work. She reads everything before anyone else and I can always tell if it's a good read by the look on her face. In the case of DeSoto, I saw a few smiles, so it must be an interesting read. My son Chris accompanied me on all of the research expeditions for this book, and the thousands of miles we trekked were certainly made better by each other's company. I hope you have as much fun reading this book as I did writing it, and it is my sincere hope that it does justice to the wonderful story of DeSoto.

As a last note, the author is fully aware of the historical impact and significance of foreign DeSotos and DeSoto trucks, and every attempt has been made to at least acknowledge the fact that they were built; however, to do justice to these two areas would require a separate book on both. This writing focuses primarily on DeSoto's U.S. production and the story behind it.

FOREWORD

By Edward Herrmann

As an enthusiast of antique cars, I was intrigued when Dennis asked me to write the foreword to a book on DeSoto. After all, I had never owned one, and the closest I had ever come to one was during my work for several years on radio and television ads for DeSoto's cousin Dodge. After some thought, several ideas came to mind about how to introduce such a book, and it then became clear that a book on one specific marque does more than just chronicle the life and death of a car company. It allows us to understand the greater subject of mechanized transportation, a subject that is hugely complex, by concentrating on only one of its many parts. And this may make it easier to understand the larger story.

The DeSoto story itself is an interesting one, and one that deserves to be told. As we grow ever distant from the foundations of the machine that literally changed the course of history, our knowledge does not come from the people that were there, but only through words and books. It is important then that we have references to these great automobile companies that shaped our lives. The formative years of the automobile are also quite different than that of the modern era. While today's automobile may use parts assembled from the global economy, a vehicle like DeSoto was purely an American effort. No metric tools, no 13-inch-diameter wheels, and no obscure name badges that are little more than bizarre hieroglyphics. One look at the graceful flying lady mascot on the hood of a DeSoto S-11 is all it takes to see that it was a different era, and moreover, a time in American automotive history that is gone and will never come back.

Which brings us to a book about the wonderful DeSoto, which is certainly needed. It provides us with a vital link to a car company that helped get us through the Great Depression, took us to the battlefields of World War II, and then retuned home to take us to the drive-in movie theater. DeSoto was a car for the American family, and that is just what Walter P. Chrysler's vision of DeSoto was. It may be gone, but the wonderful DeSoto is not forgotten. It lives on as a part of the heart and spirit of America's great automotive history.

Edward Herrmann

INTRODUCTION

It happened in a very business-like manner; there were no press conferences or banners announcing the event. Instead, in a brief memo dated November 18, 1960, the Chrysler Corporation announced that production of DeSoto would end. Although there were designs for a new model on the drawing board when the announcement was made, an American DeSoto for 1962 would never see the light of day. The styling vision of Virgil Exner, who had guided Chrysler through the latter half of the 1950s, would fall from favor, and in his stead would come Elwood Engle, a more conservative stylist who would take Chrysler styling in a different direction.

Despite the loss of DeSoto, the Chrysler Corporation would survive through the 1960s and beyond while enduring a number of ups and downs. In the present day, the company now known as DaimlerChrysler, is rich in designs, innovative in concepts, and stands on firm ground. The company that Walter P. Chrysler built is today one of the largest automobile makers in the world, but all of this success would not have happened were it not for the solid reputation of its great cars. Certainly there were a number of good cars available in the 1920s, but when Chrysler introduced the DeSoto Series K Six in mid-1928, the stage was set

for a newcomer at the table. A new face was in the crowd, and Walter P. Chrysler would do everything in his power to see that his new mid-priced DeSoto survived.

Although many Americans are aware of the vast array of companies that offer automobiles in the present day, very few are well-versed in the multitude of car manufacturers that dotted the landscape in the formative years of the motorcar. Great names like Locomobile, Duesenberg, Marmon, Stutz, and Pierce-Arrow were long ago relegated to the history books, but within the context of these forgotten giants of yesteryear there were a few that managed to survive well past the Great Depression. Names like Studebaker, Hudson, Rambler, and Packard managed to stay around just long enough to become memorable to a generation of Americans known as the baby boomers. Hot Dog stands, full-service gas stations, and drive-

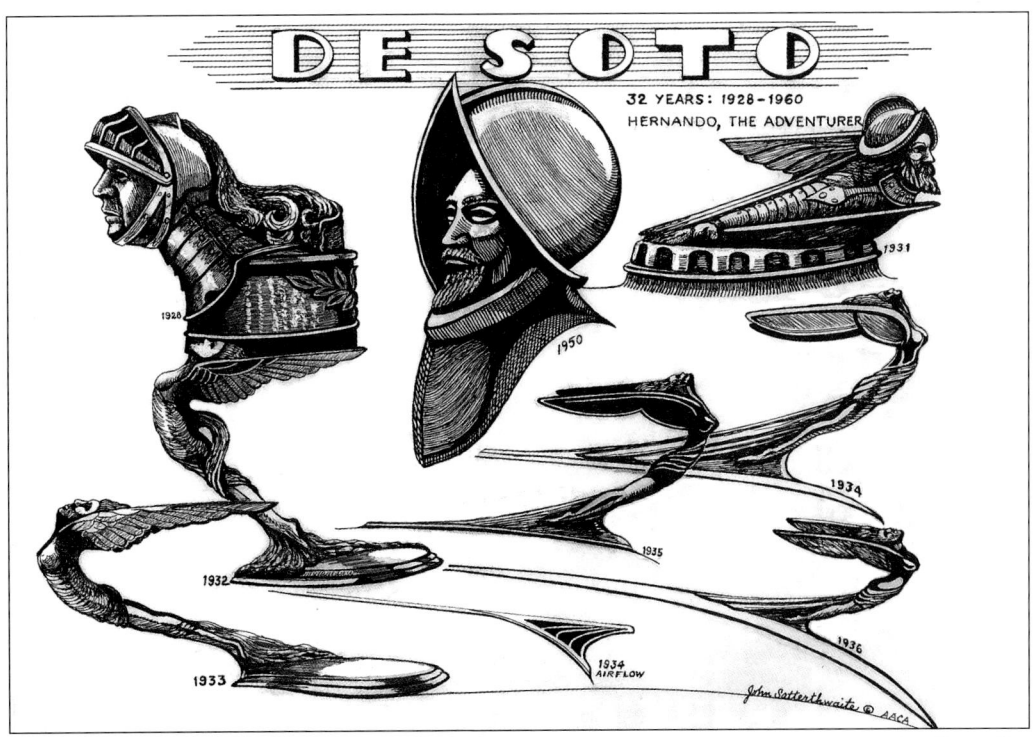

Artwork by John Satterthwaite

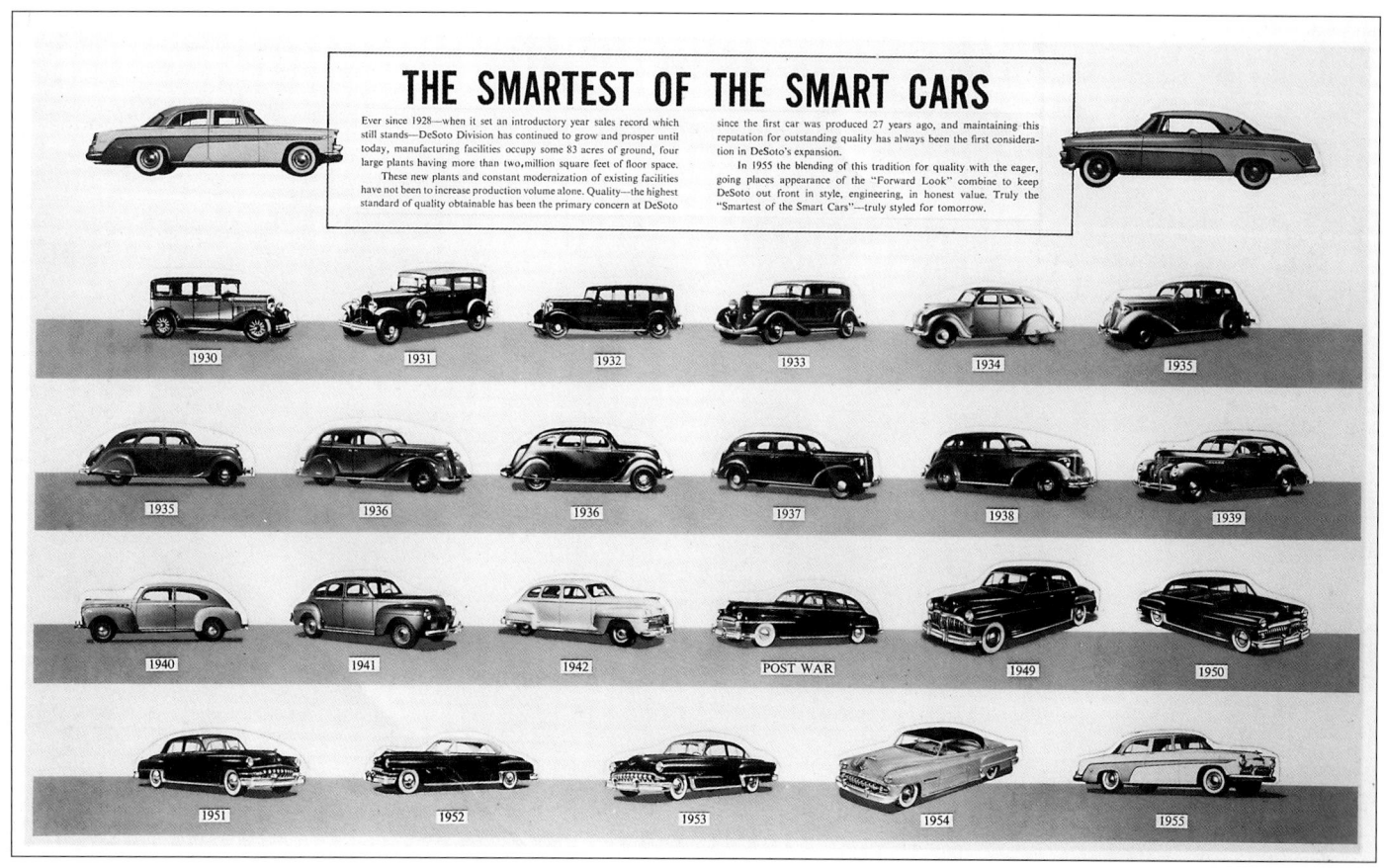

THE SMARTEST OF THE SMART CARS

Ever since 1928—when it set an introductory year sales record which still stands—DeSoto Division has continued to grow and prosper until today, manufacturing facilities occupy some 83 acres of ground, four large plants having more than two,million square feet of floor space.

These new plants and constant modernization of existing facilities have not been to increase production volume alone. Quality—the highest standard of quality obtainable has been the primary concern at DeSoto

since the first car was produced 27 years ago, and maintaining this reputation for outstanding quality has always been the first consideration in DeSoto's expansion.

In 1955 the blending of this tradition for quality with the eager, going places appearance of the "Forward Look" combine to keep DeSoto out front in style, engineering, in honest value. Truly the "Smartest of the Smart Cars"—truly styled for tomorrow.

From the Les Pesavento collection

in movie theaters are the childhood memories of this unique generation. While many of the pastimes that these children came to know and love fell by the wayside as the years went by, the memories lived on in the minds of many. So it is that many tend to find their way back to these times through vintage automobiles. With their massive amounts of chrome and flashy colors, yesterday's automobiles serve as reminders of America's dominance in the automobile market. Long before gas mileage was a major concern, and many years before the invasion of small cars from foreign lands, the American automobile stood as an icon of technology and progress. Large horsepower V-8s and fins of glory were hallmarks of the day, and Americans grew to love their cars.

The story of DeSoto is certainly an interesting one, and for the most part it is a story of success. This success can be traced not only to

Walter Chrysler himself, but also to a number of people who surrounded him. Anyone who has read of Walter Chrysler surely knows of his talent for gathering the best people, organizing production, and making things happen. His work at Buick, Willys-Overland, and Maxwell is legendary. Chrysler had a way of looking at things that took many by surprise. Today, he might be thought of as more of a manager or engineer than a "car man," but the reality is that Chrysler was a manufacturing genius. Had he lived until the year 1960, when DeSoto was taking its last breaths of life, we can only imagine one of his bookkeepers strolling into his office and explaining that the division was losing money and needed to close. His answer probably would not have been to dump millions of dollars into it in order to save it, but more likely he would have agreed with the assessment and terminated it, leaving

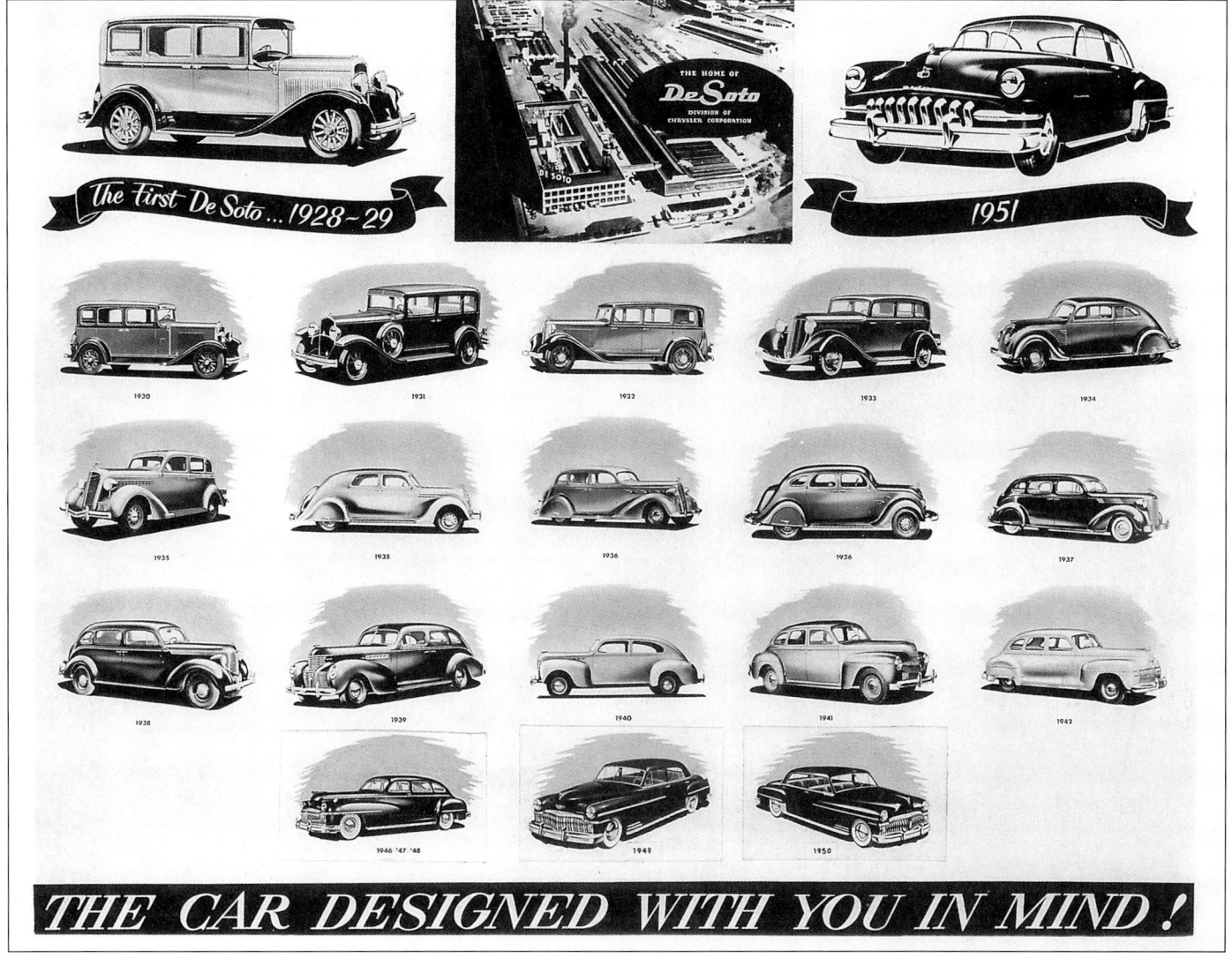

The First De Soto ... 1928~29

THE HOME OF De Soto DIVISION OF CHRYSLER CORPORATION

1951

1930 · 1931 · 1932 · 1933 · 1934

1935 · 1935 · 1936 · 1936 · 1937

1938 · 1939 · 1940 · 1941 · 1942

1946 '47 '48 · 1949 · 1950

THE CAR DESIGNED WITH YOU IN MIND!

more capital for the better performing divisions. Walter Chrysler knew how to get things done in an efficient way, and when it came to making a deal, he was a businessman. While DeSoto may have been profitable in much of its 32-year tenure, its demise, which started in the late 1950s, was a journey from which there was no return.

What then could we possibly say about DeSoto? It was a car born against the odds of the Great Depression, but still managed to set a sales record that would remain intact until the debut of the Ford Falcon three decades later. The DeSoto was billed as "a lot of car for the money," and sales proved it. When the news of

DeSoto's end came, many took sorrow in the fact that a car they had come to know and love would no longer be a part of the automotive landscape. It was as if a family member had been taken away. The DeSoto that had taken them home from the hospital, and then to their high school prom, would vanish, and with it would go the dreams of many people.

In between DeSoto's introduction in 1928 and its demise in 1960 (the last DeSoto was built in 1960 as a 1961 model) would come 32 years of wonderful styling, bright colors, and power to spare. Indeed a full generation of Americans would come to know the DeSoto as "their" car. Many DeSotos were passed on

Artwork by John Satterthwaite

to children by parents who bought them as new cars. The story also has a patriotic flavor, as DeSoto was a leader in America's defense during World War II and the Korean War. The DeSoto story is certainly one of ups and downs, but an interesting story it is.

Today, we can look back at the wonderful and rich legacy of DeSoto, a car that had something for everyone. It was a reliable car that offered solid transportation at a sensible price, and many people knew this and continued to buy DeSotos for many years. Several advertisements during DeSoto's heyday touted that seven out of ten DeSoto owners were still driving their cars many years after buying them. This testimony would play out in many forms, even as DeSoto went to war in the 1940s. The company that turned out dependable cars turned its attention to build-

ing dependable airplanes and tanks. Americans knew and respected this, and it is for this reason that DeSoto prospered until a crowded market pushed it into the annals of automotive history. This history is all we have left of this once proud automobile. Indeed the memories of DeSoto can be read in the passages of several books and magazines, and there is also a worldwide club dedicated to the marque. While an American produced DeSoto hasn't been built for many decades, they are, and forever will be, a part of American history.

This book, then, is all about the rich legacy of DeSoto. Join us now as we take a look at a company that showed America and the world how good a car could be. It's the story of a machine, but it's also the story of an American enterprise. It's Delightful, it's Delovely, it's DeSoto!

Artwork by John Satterthwaite

Chapter 1

THE BEGINNING

The success of a large company is seldom measured by the efforts of just one man, but in the case of the Chrysler Corporation; it was indeed just that. The founder of the Chrysler Corporation, Walter Percy Chrysler was a man of vision and talent, so much so that it seemed that everything he touched turned to gold. A look at his past finds his name associated with many car companies that can be considered the building blocks of the modern automobile. Buick, Willys-Overland, Chalmers, Maxwell, Plymouth, Imperial, Dodge, Fargo trucks, and, of course, DeSoto all carried the fingerprints of Chrysler's talent at one time or another. Although wealthy enough to retire at the relatively young age of 45, sitting idle while time passed by was not his way. His years at Buick had left him very well off, and Buick was also better off for his efforts, but his retirement proved short-lived. His wife, Della Forker Chrysler sensed his restlessness, and it was only a short time into his retirement that she said, "I wish you would go to work." This was the green light that Chrysler needed, and like a racehorse jumping from the starting gate, he was once again immersed in his work.

He needed a challenge, he needed a task, but most of all, he needed to prove once again that he could take something that was broken and make it work. It was from this starting point that Chrysler would go on to found the company that would bear his name, and along with that name would come DeSoto, Plymouth, Imperial, Dodge, and Fargo trucks.

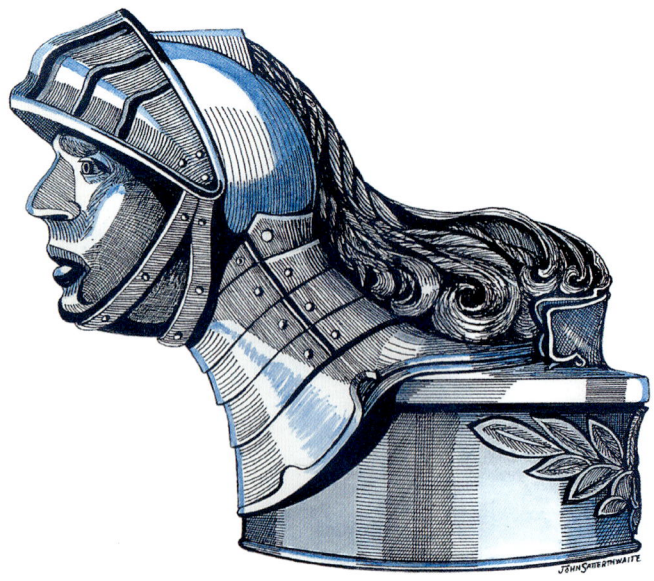

The hood mascot for the first DeSoto was a finely crafted likeness of a Spanish explorer. *Artwork by John Satterthwaite*

The first motorcar to ever bear Hernando's name was an Indiana car called the "de Soto." It remained in production for only two years. *Society of Automotive Historians, Dunwoodie Archives/ AACA Library and Research Center*

Our story of DeSoto would not be complete without a brief mention of the very first automobile to bear the famous Spanish explorer's name, which actually had nothing to do with Chrysler. Spelled "de Soto," this automobile was built in Auburn, Indiana, the home of many fine automobiles during the formative years of this new fangled contraption. The first "de Soto" was the product of the Zimmerman Company of Auburn, Indiana. The Zimmerman Company was a family run organization that entered the motorcar market in 1908. Their first car was little more than a motorized buggy, but a four-cylinder car had made its way into the line-up by 1910. By 1913, a six-cylinder car was added, but it was built as a subsidiary and simply called "de Soto." The company chose to spell Hernando's name correctly with a lower case "d," and also added a space in between the "de" and "Soto," but advertising and reviews of the car routinely confused the spelling. In any event, Zimmerman's de Soto Six lasted only two years. The deaths of several Zimmerman family members left only John Zimmerman to run the company,

and he simply chose to concentrate his efforts on a car bearing the family name. Thus, the first car to ever bear Hernando's name quietly passed into history in 1914 after a two-year production run. The de Soto name would then remain dormant until revived by Chrysler for the 1929 model year.

When Walter Chrysler introduced the Series K DeSoto Six in August of 1928, there were a few similarities between his car and the Zimmerman's. Both were introduced as a companion car to a big brother, and both were merely a way to offer a different car by using the resources of a larger enterprise. More importantly, both offered yet another car that was built to penetrate an already crowded market. The difference between Chrysler's vision of DeSoto and the Zimmerman's vision was that Walter's DeSoto had the backing of the Chrysler Corporation. With deep pockets, Chrysler was able to weather the fickle automobile market of the 1930s, and those pockets would be tested during the depths of the Great Depression. Whereas Zimmerman lacked the necessary resources to keep his de Soto afloat, Chrysler

The Chrysler Corporation depicted an image of Hernando de Soto carrying the banner of the de Soto family crest for one of its first brochures. *Society of Automotive Historians, Dunwoodie Archives/AACA Library and Research Center*

A dealer showroom in 1928 displays a beautiful setting for the new DeSoto. Note the use of exquisite lighting and flowers to brighten up the showroom. *From the Les Pesavento Collection*

was able to hang on for the long run, and his DeSoto went on to enjoy great success.

Walter Chrysler's vision of DeSoto and what it could do for America was more than just a new car for the masses. Chrysler often thought of the automobile as more than just a machine. Indeed when a car rolled off the assembly line he would not marvel at its beauty, but rather he would think of how many jobs were created by building it. When a truck was built, he would often remark that someone had to drive it, and therefore, another job was created. This was his philosophy, and this was the pioneering spirit that made Chrysler the man he was. Walter P. Chrysler was a man born into the right era at the right time. America was just waking up to the mighty industrial age. Great steam locomotives were traversing the country and in time a plethora of motorcar companies were building motorcars at incredible rates.

Chrysler first immersed himself in the business of trains, and when he had learned the train business both inside and out, he moved on to automobiles. Born into an era of self-reliance, he learned that in order to survive in the world, one had to have a trade. He cut his manufacturing teeth in the roundhouses and maintenance sheds of America's great railroads. Working for the Union Pacific; Atchison, Topeka & Santa Fe; Colorado & Southern; and the Denver & Rio Grande Western, Chrysler learned his trade and in time became one of the best locomotive mechanics in the business. His talents were in demand everywhere he went. He was making what was then considered an excellent living while working for the railroads, but a visit to the Chicago Auto Show in 1908 changed everything in his world. Mortgaging all but $700, he purchased a grand Locomobile touring car at the show for the sum of $5,000:

A first year DeSoto sedan is present while its occupants watch a landing of the famous Graf Zeppelin. The painting is by Harrison Miller. *From the Doug Dressler Collection*

a rather large amount of money in 1908. The Locomobile sat in a shed behind his house where he proceeded to take it apart and reassemble it until he completely understood its inner workings. The family's first outing in the Locomobile resulted in it being hauled out of a ditch by a team of horses. But this would not deter Chrysler, for he had seen the future, and the future was the automobile.

Chrysler had pretty much worked his way up to the top of the railroad industry when a call came from James J. Storrow, the head of Lee, Higginson & Company. Storrow was also a director of the American Locomotive Company and head of its finance committee. For a brief time, Storrow had been president of General Motors. Chrysler, who worked for American Locomotive at the same time, was unaware of Storrow as he reported only to lower levels of management. Storrow invited Chrysler to have a look around the fledgling Buick manufacturing facility, which was producing a paltry 45 cars per day. After touring the plant, Chrysler knew he could do better. Storrow instructed Chrysler to meet with Buick President Charles Nash to work out the details. Although at the time Chrysler was making an astounding $12,000 per year for ALCO, he accepted Nash's offer of $6,000 per year at Buick. The keen mind of Walter Chrysler was hard at work, for he knew in time that he could make it pay off—and pay off it did. By the time he left GM in 1919, he was being paid an astronomical $500,000 per year at a

Assembly line workers apply finishing touches to a line of sedans in 1929. Note that the lead car carries the standard artillery wheels, while the second is fitted with optional wire rims. *From the Les Pesavento Collection*

time when Henry Ford's Model T was selling for as little as $525.

So it was that Walter Chrysler began his automotive career with Buick and quickly increased production from 45 cars per day to 200. Cars were rolling off the assembly line and business was good, but in 1915 Billy Durant re-entered the corporation that was known as General Motors. Chrysler's relationship with Durant was always a "bump and grind," and Chrysler eventually left Buick due to several disagreements with Durant, who, despite be-

ing a genius, was known to be a difficult employer. Whatever his reasons for leaving Buick were, it cannot be denied that Chrysler left the company in a much better financial condition than he found it in. His plan was to retire and spend some quality time with his family. Many years of traveling with railroad jobs, and the constant travel from Detroit to New York while working for Buick, had taken place at the expense of his family. Retirement was difficult for Chrysler, for he still had tall mountains to conquer. He decided to seek new opportuni-

DE SOTO SIX

PRODUCT of CHRYSLER

Sedan de Lujo, $955 at Factory
Special equipment extra

$845
and up, at the factory

MODISH, BEAUTIFUL — and FINE THROUGHOUT

De Soto Six, despite its most moderate price, has been singled out as a fashionable car. It is fit companion for the larger, costlier cars in the most exacting homes. It rides with a richness of ease unknown in its class. It is not merely amply powered but magnificently so, and it is fine throughout. In the De Soto Six, at last high quality and moderate price are joined together.

Visit De Soto Six exhibits at Chicago Automobile Show and Congress Hotel, January 26–February 2.

DE SOTO MOTOR CORPORATION *(Division of Chrysler Corporation), Detroit, Michigan*

An ad from the February 1929 edition of *The American Magazine* displays the elegance of the DeSoto Six Sedan de Lujo. *From the Les Pesavento Collection*

ties, which he would find in the form of the Willys-Overland Company.

The chronology of Walter P. Chrysler's entrance into the company that would bear his name and eventually build the DeSoto began with his expertise in manufacturing methods. In 1920, he was approached by an old friend named Ralph Van Vechten who was the very same man that had loaned Chrysler the $4,300 he needed to buy the Locomobile back in 1908. Van Vechten represented a group of bankers concerned about their investment in the Willys-Overland Company. Willys had been on the brink of receivership for far too long, and the stockholders were worried. They approached Chrysler and negotiated a deal that put Walter Chrysler at the helm of the Willys-Overland Company. When Chrysler took over the ailing company, Willys was currently offering three cars in its line-up, and was also working on a new Willys-Knight Six secretly being developed at the former Duesenberg plant in Elizabeth, New Jersey. Three very talented men whose experience had been previously honed at Studebaker undertook the design and development of the new car. Fred Zeder, Owen Skelton, and Carl Breer were three talented engineers whose names are still talked about in automotive history circles today. It was through the efforts of these men that the Chrysler name and the DeSoto car would be carved into the annals of automobile history.

Out of all the cars in the Willys line-up, it was the Willys Six that Zeder, Skelton, and Breer were working on that intrigued Chrysler the most. As early as 1920 there were rumors in the automotive circles that the secret Willys-Knight Six would be introduced as the Chrysler Six. Chrysler had spent only two years at Willys, but in that time he had streamlined its manufacturing methods enough to stem the flow of red ink. Shortly thereafter, John North Willys was able to wrest control of his company from the bankers through a series of stock deals. But the deal also called for the Willys-Knight Six car and its New Jersey manufacturing plant to be sold at auction. Chrysler had since left Willys, not because it was now a profitable company, but because of another challenge presented to him by the holders of the Maxwell Company, which in an effort to stay alive, had recently merged with Chalmers. When the Willys-Knight Six and the entire New Jersey assembly plant was auctioned to the highest bidder Chrysler saw an opportunity and sent a representative to the auction, which was held on June 9, 1922.

A glamour photo shows the beautiful DeSoto Roadster Espanol for 1929. Base price for the Roadster was $845. This example carries optional wire wheels. *From the Les Pesavento Collection*

Chrysler's plan was to use the new Six for the Maxwell line. Unfortunately, none other than his old boss Billy Durant outbid him. This car would go on to become the Flint, which Durant would keep in production from 1923 to 1927, until he was forced to sell it to GM in order to raise the capital needed to keep his empire afloat.

While the Willys-Knight Six had slipped through his hands at the auction, Chrysler would not be detoured. He contracted the engineering talents of Zeder, Skelton, and Breer, and encouraged them to come up with a fresh design. In 1923, the three talented engineers were hard at work in the Chalmers plant in

Detroit. The Chalmers was being phased out of production, and the new car taking its place would be called the Chrysler Six.

The new Chrysler was formally introduced to the public in January 1924 and was capable of a top speed of 75 miles per hour. Bolstering its performance image was noted racecar driver Ralph DePalma, who won the Mt. Wilson Hill Climb in a new Chrysler. DePalma then drove the very same car 1,000 miles in 1,007 minutes at the Fresno, California, board track, setting a new stock car racing record in the process. This kind of publicity helped put the new Chrysler on the map, and after only two years of production Chrysler began contemplating

The Hernando de Soto family crest was carried on the radiator for 1929. *Society of Automotive Historians, Dunwoodie Archives/AACA Library and Research Center*

an expansion of the company's offerings. It was around this time that Chrysler realized that he might be able to build a company big enough to compete with Ford and General Motors.

For 1927, Chrysler offered a series of four cars including the four-cylinder Model I-50, which was little more than a leftover Maxwell. For 1928, this car would be renamed Plymouth, with the first one rolling off the assembly line on June 11, 1928. Although not introduced until June, Plymouth would sell 58,000 cars by the end of the year. After many years of success with the famous Model T, Henry Ford now faced the realization that he did not own the low-priced automobile market.

It was clear that the Plymouth could compete in the low-priced car market very well, and Chrysler's Series H-60 and "Finer" 70

models would carry the mid-priced market. In a class by itself was the E-80 Series Imperial, which was Chrysler's top-of-the-line model. All of these different models under one roof did have a purpose, for this was the era of the companion car. Cadillac had the LaSalle, Oakland had the Pontiac, Hudson had the Essex, and even high-end Marmon produced a car named the Roosevelt. All of these cars were built to offer competition in the various pricing levels of the market. At Chrysler, the Series 80 Imperial was intended to challenge the luxury market dominated by such cars as Cadillac, Pierce-Arrow, and Packard, but Chrysler itself offered the Series 52, 62, and 72, with prices running from $670 to $3,595, thereby aiming at several different marques. Construction of a new car from Chrysler would certainly help

While others had the sedan, DeSoto had the Sedan de Lujo. Wood artillery wheels were standard. *Society of Automotive Historians, Dunwoodie Archives/AACA Library and Research Center*

define Chrysler's place in the market, and the DeSoto would do just that.

Chrysler's new company was performing well beyond everyone's expectations, but its manufacturing capacity was now being severely tested. Chrysler had also introduced a commercial car and truck line, which strained the company's production facilities to the absolute limits. What Walter Chrysler needed was more manufacturing space, more machines, and most of all, a foundry where he could cast his own parts. He was in danger of becoming over-expanded, and this is why the Dodge Brothers foundries had an attraction that Chrysler found hard to resist. In 1927, the Dodge Brothers Company was held by the New York banking company of Dillon, Read, & Company, who wished to divest itself of the automobile business. On July 31, 1928, Walter Chrysler purchased Dodge for $170 million in stock..

While Walter Chrysler was in negotiations with the bankers that held Dodge, he was also developing a new six-cylinder car aimed directly at the medium-priced field. Ironically enough, that medium-priced field consisted of a plethora of cars, which included Dodge. Thus, the Dodge Brothers car that Walter Chrysler was buying was a similar car that he was already prepared to do battle with in the mid-priced market. This new car was called DeSoto. Some have speculated that Chrysler actually developed the DeSoto in order to prod Dillon, Read & Company into selling their stock. A quote from Chrysler executive K. T. Keller lends support to this theory. Walter

The DeSoto Faeton weighed in at 2,445 pounds, and was a great car for the family. The Faeton was the only model to use a two-piece windshield for 1929. *Society of Automotive Historians, Dunwoodie Archives/AACA Library and Research Center*

Chrysler had approached Keller in 1926 and lamented that Dodge was in trouble and could possibly be bought. What Walter Chrysler wanted was Dodge's manufacturing and distribution infrastructure and the introduction of DeSoto would certainly apply pressure on Dillon, Read & Company to sell. Chrysler even hired the Dodge Brothers' sales manager in order to play down the reliability of Dodge and talk up the wonders of Chrysler. The negotiations of Chrysler's acquisition of Dodge were tense, and Walter Chrysler was brutal, but the deal went through. Chrysler purchased Dodge, and DeSoto was introduced just four days later. When the deal with Dodge was signed, Chrysler could have simply chosen to scrap the DeSoto, as the Dodge would have filled the medium-priced market nicely, but Chrysler let production of the DeSoto go forward. With the DeSoto selling for just under the price of a new Dodge, Walter Chrysler felt sure that the two divisions would somehow balance out and find their place in the market. History would show that these two cars would be considered twins with a close family lineage.

Corporate structure for Chrysler's new DeSoto division was well defined, and a good

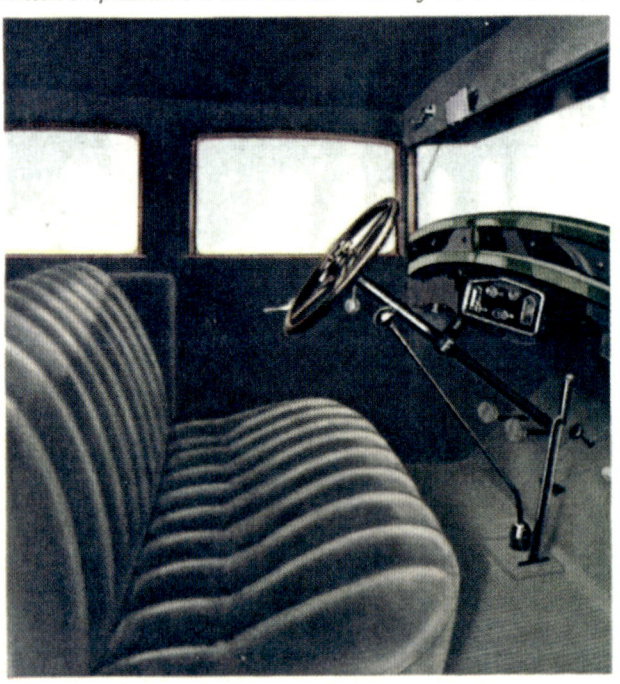

Unusual roominess, well-placed controls, comfortably shaped seats and genuine mohair upholstery are qualities which emphasize the unmatched value of the De Soto Six.

DeSoto interiors were smartly designed with plenty of room, genuine mohair upholstery, and easy-to-read gauges. *Society of Automotive Historians, Dunwoodie Archives/AACA Library and Research Center*

The 1930 Series CK Roadster was a handsome car. This example was built in Detroit and shipped to Australia, then returned to the U.S. during the 1980s. Note the right-hand drive. *Photo by Dennis David*

team managed the division effectively. Joe Fields served as president of the DeSoto Motor Corporation, and C. W. Matheson was vice president of sales. Bertram Hutchinson was named vice president and treasurer, and Chrysler, himself, was the chairman. Chief engineering duties fell to James Zeder, who handled the job for both the DeSoto and Plymouth divisions. James Zeder was the younger brother of Fred, one of the talented engineers that helped get the company started with the

first Chrysler. With all of the elements in place, DeSoto was ready to make its mark.

The introduction of the DeSoto Series K on August 6, 1928, caused quite a stir with the American motoring public. More than 500 dealers signed up to distribute the new car immediately, and the dealer network increased to 1,500 by the end of the year. So successful was the new DeSoto that it set a previously unheard of sales record for a new automobile. Within its first year over 80,000 were on the road. In hindsight, we only have to look at the car itself for the reason why; quite simply, it was a beautiful car. Named after a legendary Spanish explorer, the DeSoto's image spoke of a car that could go anywhere. Its styling attributes were pleasing as well. Riding on a 109.75-inch wheelbase, the Series K featured a triple set of vertical hood louvers, an arched headlamp tie-bar, and a set of lamps integral with the cowl molding. The DeSoto's front-end appearance had an air of class that spoke of the finer automobiles of the day. Standard equipment included a Delco-Remy ignition system, Lovejoy shock absorbers, and Lockheed hydraulic brakes.

The new Series K also added an image of class and elegance with its alluring new model names. While other car companies were offering a coupe, DeSoto had the Cupe de Lujo, the sedan was called the Sedan Coche, and the fabulous roadster was called the Roadster Espanol. In total, there were seven different models to choose from and each was well appointed both inside and out. Selling for under $1,000, the buyer of a new DeSoto got a lot of car for the money. Attractive looks and extraordinary reliability were the hallmarks of the new car. Not since Harley Earl's design work on Cadillac's new LaSalle in 1927 had the motoring public seen a more glamorous car. DeSoto's introductory year production of over 80,000 cars set a record that would stand for a full 31 years, and would not be broken until Ford's introduction of the Falcon in 1960.

A 1929 DeSoto Series K Sedan de Lujo was a smart buy for the motoring public. Priced at just $885, the Sedan de Lujo offered excellent reliability and plenty of room. *From the Les Pesavento Collection*

A DeSoto Roadster Espanol sports optional wire wheels and the rare hood mascot. *From the Doug Dressler Collection*

Chapter 2

MOVING FORWARD

After grabbing the attention of the motoring public, DeSoto immediately began setting the pace for others to follow. For 1930, its second year in production, another six-cylinder car called the Series CK was offered, and a Series CF carried an eight-cylinder. Drawing 70 horsepower from a 207.7-cubic-inch block, the DeSoto Eight was capable of spectacular performance. The DeSoto Eights and Sixes were easily distinguished by the vertical hood louver arrangement. The Six retained its standard grouping of three sets, while the Eight featured undivided hood louvers running down the sides from front to back. DeSoto's model year designation for 1930 actually occurred in August 1929, with cars built, thereafter, known as First Series 1930 models. It was during the latter half of 1929 that DeSoto built its 100,000[th] car as a 1930 model. DeSoto had now firmly established itself as a solid entry in the mid-priced field of automobiles. The U.S. economy was still coming to terms with the Great Depression, and the Chrysler Corporation positioned itself to withstand the tough times ahead.

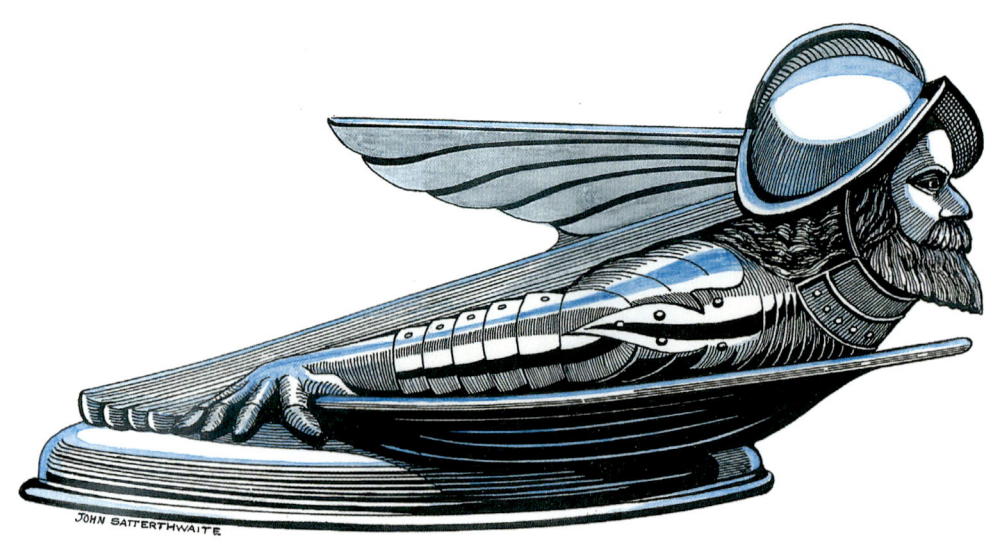

DE SOTO
1931 MASCOT

A redesigned bust of Hernando de Soto himself was available for 1931. It was an extra cost option. *Artwork by John Satterthwaite*

The big news for DeSoto's second year was eight-cylinder power in the CF Series. Advertising touted the fact that the average motorist could now step up to an eight-cylinder previously reserved for the higher echelons of society. *From the Les Pesavento Collection*

By the early 1930s, the Chrysler Corporation was on firm ground with offerings in every segment of the market, and was considered a formidable contender in the automobile market. From his humble beginnings in the small town of Ellis, Kansas, Walter Chrysler had managed to build a corporation that could compete with the likes of General Motors. The new DeSoto had become a dominating force in the mid-priced field, but there was more to come. The next three decades would find the DeSoto name a benchmark of solid transportation. Walter Chrysler had achieved what many others could only have dreamed of: he had created a car for every price level of the market.

The stock market crash of October 29, 1929, saw millions of Americans financially drained of everything they owned. The depression caused a shift in sales to lower priced cars and despite the darkness and gloom that surrounded the industry Chrysler managed to survive

After just 14 months in production, DeSoto built its 100,000th car. *From the Les Pesavento Collection*

the turbulent economic times. Versatility was the key to Chrysler's survival, and a multitude of different models and engines offered motorists several choices in every price range. Indeed the Chrysler Corporation's plethora of engines was mind-boggling with overlaps of cubic-inch displacements, cylinders, and horsepower. With so many engines available, it became abundantly evident that streamlining the company's engine offerings could save dollars. Six-cylinder offerings were reduced from seven to five, and two new eight-cylinder engines were now offered in the 1930 line-up. This was in direct response to competition in the late 1920s, which had seen Packard, Hupmobile, Nash, Studebaker, and several others offering eight-cylinder cars. Chrysler had forecast the need for an eight-cylinder engine a few years earlier, and Fred Zeder had begun work on a new design in 1927. This new eight-cylinder engine was ready for the 1930 model year.

Following the standard manufacturing methods used at the time, DeSoto actually built First and Second Series cars within the calendar year.

DeSoto's marketing campaign featured ads written directly to women. Copywriter Helen Brown extolled the virtues of DeSoto's style and comfort in this advertisement that features a country club setting. *From the Les Pesavento Collection*

First Series cars were introduced in June and production ran until December. Second Series cars were introduced in January and production ran through June, whereupon the next year's models would prevail. This production schedule would continue until 1932, when DeSoto's accounting for new cars would change over to a single model per year running (roughly) concurrent with the calendar year. Production figures were kept only by model and not by year. Thus, prior to 1932, a First and Second Series DeSoto would have combined production totals accounting for all cars built within the model year from June through May of the following year. With four different marques available from the Chrysler Corporation, this new method of accounting helped to streamline operations and avoid the considerable confusion generated by so many different models. The only exception to this new accounting method would occur immediately following World War II, when production of the Series S-11 would continue uninterrupted for three years while DeSoto fed a car-starved public.

Unique styling of the DeSoto CF's dashboard featured easily read gauges and simple controls. In later years, DeSotos would be known for their beautiful dashboards that featured vast amounts of brightwork and color. *From the Les Pesavento Collection*

For 1930, the Series K was carried over essentially unchanged, but a new CK model was introduced in May of that year. While both the DeSoto and Plymouth were built at the same plant, the new CK borrowed many parts from its cousin Plymouth. Billed as the new "Finer Six," the CK featured a few mechanical refinements that made it a stellar performer. Using the Silver Dome engine, the cylinder bore was increased by an eighth of an inch, a bigger carburetor was fitted, and a new manifold had rounded corners for better airflow. The CK's body shared the same look as Plymouth's Model 30-U.

Eight-cylinder engines were in vogue for 1930 and DeSoto's Series CF would carry the banner for this new trend. Although built at the same DeSoto/Plymouth Highland Park

plant as the K and CK Series, the CF did not utilize parts from its little brothers. Instead, it used many parts from Dodge, which was nearby. This was made possible because Dodge was also using the new eight-cylinder engine, and these were the first Chrysler products to use eights. Historians have often speculated as to why an eight-cylinder power plant was not reserved for the upper line Imperial, which was still chugging along with an L-Head Six for 1930. DeSoto's new CF Eight rode on a 114-inch wheelbase and used semi-elliptic springs with an I-beam front axle. A rigid seven-cross-member frame ensured stability on all roads, and stopping power came from four-wheel hydraulic brakes with 11-inch drums supplied by Lockheed. The new CF Eight featured a 207.7-cubic-inch L-Head design that generated a respectable 70 horsepower. With many competitors also fielding low-priced eights, the CF was an attempt to keep up with the market, which it did quite well. Selling for $965 in the Business Coupe body style, the DeSoto CF Eight was able to undercut Marmon's Roosevelt by just enough dollars to be proclaimed the lowest priced eight-cylinder car on the market. The most expensive DeSoto CF for the 1930 model year was the Convertible Coupe selling for $1,075.

As with most of the industry, the Great Depression was not kind to DeSoto, and had it not been for its unprecedented startup at introduction there was the chance that it might have been eliminated from the Chrysler family line altogether. In March 1930, the Chrysler Corporation made the best of the fact that the depression was shifting the motoring public's interest to lower priced cars. Plymouth, which was now a division of its own after previously being sold only through Chrysler dealers, expanded to Dodge and DeSoto dealerships as well. This increased Plymouth's dealership structure to over 7,000 outlets, thus ensuring

Hollywood movie actress Lina Basquette (1907-1994) was known for surrounding herself with only the best. Here she uses a DeSoto Series SA Six Roadster. Her autograph states, "A Car that Fulfills a Woman's Desire for Beauty." *Compliments of Doug Dressler from the John A. Conde Collection*

the survival of the corporation. As the Great Depression continued its icy grip on America in 1931, no industry would feel its pinch more than the automobile companies. Sales were down for virtually all of Detroit's automakers, and there were bargains to be had everywhere. The focus of most car builders began to turn from profits to mere survival, but Walter Chrysler had a different vision, as he pressed onward with several new ideas. One of those ideas was a design concept submitted by Carl Breer for a streamlined body. Chrysler gave

Breer the green light for the design, and this design culminated into the Chrysler Airflow for 1934.

The DeSoto Series CK-Six and CF-Eight were carried over from 1930 and marketed as early 1931 models with only very minor modifications. In January, DeSoto also introduced the new SA Series at the New York Auto Show. The SA bore a strong resemblance to its cousin Plymouth, but featured the 205-cubic-inch L-Head Six. In Roadster form, the SA represented a design that was as pretty as

DeSoto's 1930 Model CK Finer Six Convertible Coupe rode on a 109-inch wheelbase and featured a 60-horsepower engine. *From the Doug Dressler Collection*

a car could be. Riding on a new double-drop frame and featuring a longer hood, the new design had a smoother overall appearance that marked the beginning of a relationship between DeSoto and Plymouth that set a pattern for many years to come. DeSoto was always sharing characteristics with other Chrysler family members. DeSotos built for export carried different model names, and in future years DeSoto even offered several crossbred models for export known as Diplomats. There were years when Plymouth bodies would wear the DeSoto name, and there were even years when DeSotos would wear Dodge sheet metal.

Whether it was Plymouth, Dodge, or Chrysler, DeSoto would carry a few mechanical parts or body components from its cousins throughout its existence. This pattern would prevail all the way through DeSoto's demise in 1960. DeSoto was built on the Chrysler assembly line during its last two years of production.

The new DeSoto SA 2-door sedan was priced at just $695 for 1931, making it the lowest priced six-cylinder model ever offered by Chrysler. Standard equipment included wire wheels, exterior sun visor, hydraulic shock absorbers, and gauges for fuel and engine temperatures. It was a lot of car for $695, and the

A factory drawing of the 1931 DeSoto SA sedan shows its smart styling. The SA rode on a 109-inch wheelbase and sold for $775. *From the Doug Dressler Collection*

SA accounted for the majority of DeSoto's production. Export DeSotos also found favor. An article dated April 10, 1931, in the British publication *The Autocar,* summed up the DeSoto Eight, "Altogether, a sound car with a satisfying, easy performance, which gives of its best to the average driver with a minimum of skill in control."

DeSoto production of the SA for 1931 was moved from Chrysler's plant to the Highland Park plant previously used by Plymouth. An innovative design feature was introduced that year in the Plymouth line that would eventually find its way to the rest of the Chrysler

family. Formally known as "Floating Power" the engine was mounted low at the rear and higher up towards the front, thereby dampening the vibration that normally occurred with an in-line engine. All mounting points used rubber bushings. "Floating Power" would be introduced in the DeSoto line for 1932.

In mid-1931, the DeSoto SA Six and the CF Eight quietly assumed status as 1932 models with a few minor modifications. A new Easy-Shift transmission was now offered, along with "free wheeling," a feature that allowed the wheels to turn free and independent of the engine when the car was decelerating. This

Eight-cylinder power would disappear for DeSoto after 1931, and would not reappear until 1952. This is a Model CF Sedan, which cut a very imposing profile. *From the Doug Dressler Collection*

feature could be somewhat nerve-wracking for some motorists, since the compression braking normally used to steady the car was gone once the accelerator pedal was lifted and the car coasted as if in neutral. The big star for 1932, however, was the new DeSoto Model SC, which featured a radiator design, taken directly from the famed Miller racecars. Nothing sells cars better than fame and DeSoto enlisted the help of such noted characters as Robert Ripley (Ripley's Believe It or Not) and legendary race-car driver Peter De Paolo in 1932. De Paolo drove a new SC on a cross-country journey to-taling 3,000 miles over a period of 10 days. As if this grueling endurance run was not enough, De Paolo ended the trip with a 300-mile track run that saw the SC average nearly 80 miles per hour. This was more than enough to prove the new SC's reliability. The SC even made its way to Great Britain in 1933, being sold as the Chrysler Mortlake Six. With the introduction of the SC, DeSoto offered the widest array of models in its history (to date) with availability of many different body styles. According to a

January 9, 1932, article in the *New York Automotive Daily News*, colors for DeSoto's 1932 models wore glamorous names like Iceland Green, Maxfield Parish Blue, Everglades Red, Jack Pine Gray, and Rubicelle Maroon.

For all its beauty and durability, the SC should have been a fantastic seller, but the SA model overshadowed it, and its cousin Plymouth eventually outsold DeSoto. Perhaps this is where we find the very seed of DeSoto's ultimate demise. With the Great Depression still holding a firm grip on the U.S. economy, dealers were touting the low price of its more affordable cousin, Plymouth. In theory, Plymouth's success may have occurred at DeSoto's expense, and the Chrysler family of cars seemed to feature a misfit. However, de-

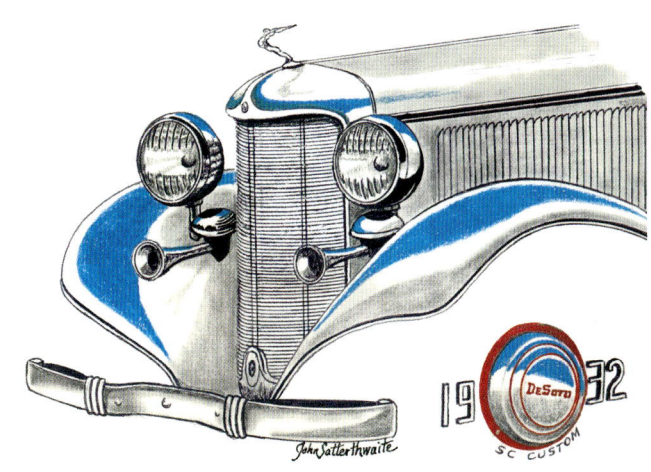

Although eight-cylinder power had been dropped for the 1932 model year, DeSoto's styling for the SC Series was inspired by the famed Miller racecars. *Artwork by John Satterthwaite*

An elegant home is the perfect setting for the new DeSoto Six convertible in this factory photo. Note the two fashionable young ladies admiring the stylish automobile. *From the Doug Dressler Collection*

A 1932 DeSoto SC Custom made for a spectacular town car. Chrysler employed its own custom body department from 1931 through 1935, and very few of these were ever built. *From the Doug Dressler Collection*

spite the tanked U.S. economy, DeSoto still managed to finish in ninth place for the 1932 calendar year, although this was due in part to the losses suffered by other companies whose financial woes were more severe than that of DeSotos.

Marketing for 1933 carried the slogan "Smartness at the Lowest Price," and an all-new DeSoto greeted buyers for 1933. Instead of allying itself with its cousin Plymouth, DeSoto would now carry parts from the Chrysler Model CC Six and Royal Model CT Eight. Introduced as the Model SD, it did not surpass sales of the previous SC, but its unique grille

treatment made it a standout in the crowd. The SD was the fourth "all-new" DeSoto in as many years, and research and development costs for DeSoto were offset by the fact that it shared many of its mechanical and body components with whichever cousin it was riding with at the time. Once again, DeSoto was using parts from the Chrysler family of cars. New features for the SD were a combination accelerator and starter pedal and a silent three-speed transmission. Another unique feature was a Flex-Beam headlamp that allowed the driver's side headlamp to be angled downward when another car approached. The passenger-

The hood mascot that graced the SC Series featured a beautifully styled goddess with wings. DeSoto would also use a variation of this theme for the S-11 Series immediately after World War II. *Artwork by John Satterthwaite*

side headlamp remained steady in order to illuminate the road straight ahead.

In June of 1933, DeSoto production was moved to Chrysler's East Jefferson Avenue plant. This was due to a combination of factors, the first of which was the fact that the SD shared parts with Chrysler. The second reason was that it allowed Plymouth to take full advantage of its own production facilities, thereby increasing Plymouth's output. Before the year was out, Plymouth would also open a second plant in Los Angeles in order to meet demand. Although the new SD was certainly a handsome car, it was not alone in its class. Indeed the SD was squarely in the middle of a rather crowded market for a car of its type.

First let's talk about "FLOATING POWER"

THERE'S no doubt in my mind that Floating Power engine mountings are the greatest contribution to the automobile in a decade. But their effect is so revolutionary that few people understand what they *really* do for the car.

Maybe this will explain it.

If you get on a horse, and the horse bounces . . . what happens? Well, you bounce, too. Or perhaps you call it posting.

But now! Take that same horse, hitch him to a buggy, sit in the buggy seat and say giddap! What happens now?

Does the horse bounce? Yes. Do you bounce? No. That's the effect of Floating Power mountings. It's the same result. The engine is moving in the frame just as the horse moves between the shafts of the buggy. *None of the engine's vibration gets back to you in the driver's seat or to anyone else seated in the car.*

In an automobile without Floating Power, the engine is mounted directly on the frame. When the engine vibrates, so does the car body. That's what has made long rides tiresome.

But with Floating Power . . . the engine *is supported at only two points . . . on special rubber mountings.*

It rocks back and forth on its own axis, *and no vibration gets back to you.*

In an attempt to explain the "Floating Power" concept to the motoring public, DeSoto ads for 1933 used a horse and buggy in order to explain the vibration-dampening engine mountings. *From the Leroy Cole Collection*

Competing with the likes of Hudson, Nash, Terraplane, Hupmobile, and even its cousin Dodge, DeSoto struggled in a market that was crowded with offerings but short of buyers. The year 1933 would turn out to be a less productive year than 1932, with only 24,496 DeSotos built for the model year. Clearly, DeSoto needed something new in order to bolster its sales.

The effects of the Great Depression were felt by the general public and businesses alike, but Walter Chrysler was always a bit more optimistic than most people. All through the Great Depression, he never cut engineering, or research and development projects. Walter Chrysler was always planning ahead and would not allow the economic factors of the depression to affect the future of the Chrysler Corporation. It is for this reason that Chrysler was able to introduce a new car for 1934. A whirlwind of publicity would precede the new car. It would be a design that was so revolutionary that nothing like it had ever before been seen. The year 1934 would bring a revolutionary new concept to American automotive styling called the Airflow.

PICTURE YOURSELF HERE

THE NEW DESOTO STANDARD 4-DOOR SEDAN

Anyone could be proud of this car. It's a style leader anywhere —anytime. We learned last year how many, how very many of America's smartest families bought DeSotos. Picture *yourself* and *your* family in this smart Standard 4-Door Sedan. Picture this car on *your* street in front of *your* house. You'll be proud . . . who wouldn't be? . . . and more, *you'll be thrifty, too!*

An ad for a DeSoto Series SD invites potential customers to "picture" themselves behind the wheel of the stylish 4-door sedan. Note the formal elegance of the background. *From the Leroy Cole Collection*

SAVING MONEY is always smart!

OLD cars are always a risk and a liability. When they get old . . . they get expensive. Repair bills mount . . . and you can never be sure when the next "break-down" will occur. That, more than anything, will cause thousands of people to buy new cars this year. *It's real economy!*

It's cars like the new DeSoto that are curing people of spending big money on new cars. Just look at a DeSoto. It gives you everything "expensive" cars used to . . . and more. It makes you smart . . . and keeps you thrifty. Saving money is always in style, and more so today than ever.

Advertising for 1933 was playing directly into the concept of saving money in repairs by buying a new car; something only very few people could do in 1933. A DeSoto SD is in the background for this shot. *From the Leroy Cole Collection*

Let a SPEED KING tell you
the mechanical features

Peter De Paolo, former holder of World's 500-Mile Speed Record.

"I MAKE a living driving cars. It's my job to take 'em out on the road and see what they'll do. They call us 'testers.' We punish cars, we race cars, and we *wreck 'em*. When we get through, and the engineers check results and act accordingly, you've got a car that can stand a lot.

"I know from experience what this new DeSoto will do. I know what's inside it. That's what I want to talk about . . . mechanical features!

"You want speed . . . DeSoto's sure got it. I've hit this car up to 85 an hour on a race track. This car goes faster than 999 out of 1000 drivers will ever want to drive.

"You want power . . . DeSoto's got '79 horse' . . . believe me, it's a puller. I've shot it up some of the toughest hills in the country in high gear . . . and it simply ate 'em up.

"And no matter where you go, it's a thrill to drive it. It's got snap and pep on the getaway . . . you can sprint through traffic or hold it wide open on a country road with so little effort the car seems to be driving itself.

"Why are these things true? Because of DeSoto's mechanical features. Let me briefly describe the 'things' that give DeSoto its safety, its performance and effortless driving. Please follow me, point by point.

Racecar driver Peter De Paolo expounded on the virtues of DeSoto for a 1933 brochure. De Paolo used several pages to explain DeSoto's mechanical refinements. *From the Leroy Cole Collection*

In this ad entitled, "LET'S GO PLACES SMARTLY," DeSoto was attempting to expound on the virtues of economy, styling, and reliability, all in the same package. *From the Leroy Cole Collection*

Chapter 3

AIRFLOWS TO AIRPLANES

Big plans were in the works for DeSoto in 1933. Walter Chrysler felt he had seen the future in Carl Breer's design of the Airflow. For 1934, DeSoto would introduce this new and radical style designated as the Series SE. It was a car that was way ahead of its time, and the general public took an immediate shine to the new style. But frustration mounted and orders were canceled when deliveries were not forthcoming. While there was a Chrysler Airflow design for 1934, the Chrysler line-up also featured the CA and CB Series, which were more conventionally styled cars. This fact left DeSoto with the lone Series SE Airflow for a market that was still mired in the Great Depression. Although the Airflow would not prove popular in the long run, history has shown it to be a good car that was mechanically advanced—its innovative design roomy and comfortable.

In preparation for the introduction of the Airflow, the Chrysler Corporation contracted with the Aero-Dynamics Company of New York City to build a car that would demon-

DeSoto introduced a radical new design called the Airflow for 1934. Officially known as the SE, it was a car that was way ahead of its time. *Artwork by John Satterthwaite*

DeSoto regularly used famous celebrities to promote its cars. In this photo, actress Ethel Merman (1908-1984) poses by a 1934 SE Airflow. As paint technology improved, paints gained a better shine in the 1930s. Note the reflection of the front fender in the door. *From the Les Pesavento Collection*

strate the benefits of an Airflow design. Believing that the blunt end of an object should ultimately be the direction of its travel, a conventionally styled 1933 DeSoto Custom was retrofitted with its driver's seat facing to the rear and all steering, acceleration, and braking controls positioned so that it could be driven backwards. In a remarkable publicity stunt, racecar driver Harry Hartz drove the strange DeSoto from Michigan to New York. It was boasted that an additional 20 percent in top speed was possible by the changing aerody-

namics of driving backwards. The test car was also stripped of all its DeSoto markings in order to create curiosity about its origins. In a move that was several years ahead of its time, the unmarked DeSoto featured a wraparound rear window similar to what GM would offer on their front panoramic windshield in 1954. Headlamps were also fitted to the rear of the car, and several publicity stunts were staged along the way so that newsreel cameras could pick up the story. The entire marketing campaign was designed specifically to let the mo-

A 1934 Series SE Airflow is nicely posed in this elegant photo. All told, 13,940 Airflows were built for the 1934 model year. *From the Doug Dressler Collection*

toring public know that something new was in the works at Chrysler and that 1934 would witness the introduction of the Airflow.

The U.S. economy was still caught up in the Great Depression in 1934, and along with the stagnant economy came a few problems. There were many car builders who had been struggling, but were now operating on life-support and would, indeed, fold before the decade was out. Among these were such greats as Duesenberg, Stutz, and Marmon. Another major factor was a growing labor movement that forced many carmakers to unionize all of their shops. The unionization of the Chrysler

Corporation, and GM, occurred in 1937. But the unionization of the automobile industry was not without conflict, and the lone holdout in the industry was Henry Ford. After a bloody battle at Ford's Rouge plant on May 26, 1937, Ford spent the next five years battling union efforts and did not give in until 1941. The conflict itself was said to be one of the most troubling incidents in Henry Ford's life. His submission to the union's demands was said to occur only after his wife Clara pleaded with him to do so. The signing of the Ford contract marked the dominance of unionization in the American automobile industry.

The Series SE became the Series SG for 1935, and a more conventional radiator grille was featured. The new grille was moved forward thereby giving the front end a more conventional look. *From the Les Pesavento Collection*

The Airflow design for 1934 can certainly be regarded as the most radical style ever carried by a DeSoto in its 32-year tenure. With rear passenger seating riding a full 20 inches in front of the rear axle, and the front seat able to accommodate three adults, the Airflow's ride was like no other. The Airflow used a conventional frame, but a series of beams and trusses gave the car a degree of strength and rigidity that was previously unheard of in an automobile. In a televised stunt that has been played over and over through the years, an Airflow was rolled down a 110-foot cliff in Pennsylvania, and then driven off under its own power. The DeSoto Airflow Series SE, and Chrysler Airflow Series CU were cars that were way ahead of their time, but the motoring public was not ready for a car of such radical innovation. The Airflow design did manage to win the coveted Grand Prix Award for aerodynamic styling in the Concours d' Elegance at Monte Carlo in 1934 and again in 1935.

Historians generally agree that there are a number of factors that contributed to the

VOTED MOST *Beautiful*

The Airflow De Soto was the undisputed Style Leader in 1934. Europe gave it the most coveted of all motor car awards —the Grand Prix in the "Concours d'Elegance" at Monte Carlo. The Airflow competed against other leading American and European automobiles.

DeSoto advertising clearly displayed an air of class and elegance for the Airflow. This ad makes mention of the Airflow receiving the coveted Grand Prix Award for Styling at Monte Carlo. *From the Les Pesavento Collection*

Airflow's failure in the market. According to National DeSoto Club member Les Pesavento, "The Airflow's demise was caused by its different aerodynamic design, and the public was not ready for its advanced styling." Another factor that contributed to sluggish sales of the new Airflow was the fact that after much hype and publicity surrounding its introduction, they were slow in getting to the dealer's showrooms. The Airflow's radical design mandated that it used several unconventional manufacturing methods, and this caused delays in getting the assembly line up and running. The unconventional manufacturing methods also forced Chrysler to raise prices for the Airflow by approximately 22 percent, which was a little

hard to swallow for a nation trying to emerge from the Great Depression. The Airflow's front-end design was also a bit more than the general public could handle. In an era of tall radiators sporting great hood mascots, the sloping design of the Airflow did not project an image of grandeur.

Indeed the same factors of a new and different front-end design would also doom the Edsel in the late 1950s. Between the delivery problems and unconventional styling, the Airflow was a car that found few buyers for 1934. Despite the fact that it was a better year for the auto industry in general, DeSoto would be the only member of the Chrysler family to lose sales over the previous year. DeSoto's Airflow

The last Airflow would come in 1936 with the Series S-2. A new grille once again graced the front end, and there were new bumpers and body side moldings. Only 5,000 units would leave the factory in the Airflow's last year. *Photo by Dennis David/2005 National DeSoto convention. St. Catherines, Ontario Canada*

would be offered in only one series with no DeLuxe or Custom Series. Indeed, when all of the totals were calculated, Plymouth would be ranked third in the industry for 1934, and DeSoto would rank a dismal 13th, building only 13,940 cars for the model year.

It was around this time that Chrysler recognized the need for expansion in foreign markets after rival Ford had introduced a pickup truck based on a car chassis in 1934. An export Plymouth was built for the Australian market that farmers were able to use for both work and pleasure. Known formally as Utility vehicles, they quickly became known as "UTEs" by Australians. Plymouth would continue to offer different models for export, and DeSoto would offer its own companion car after World War II, called the Diplomat, to

dealers outside North America. Throughout its many years with DeSoto, the Diplomat was a foreign version of a DeSoto that was based on a Plymouth or Dodge depending on the year. Diplomats were available in South Africa, Australia, and many parts of Europe. The Spanish origins of the DeSoto name resulted in good sales of Diplomats in many Spanish-speaking countries.

The Airflow was carried over into 1935, but was now designated as the Series SG. The SG featured a redesigned hood that projected a more conventional theme with a sharp V-shape defining its appearance. Due to the dismal showing of the Airflow in the market, DeSoto also introduced the new Series SF Airstream, a car of more conventional styling. The Airstream was pieced together with parts

After the disappointing sales figures of the Airflow, DeSoto introduced the conventionally styled Airstream Series SF for 1935. *From the Les Pesavento Collection*

already on the shelves of its cousins Plymouth and Dodge. The SF's only distinction was its grille, a set of long hood louvers, decorative trim, and interior appointments unique to DeSoto. Pricing for the Airstream was in-between Dodge and Chrysler, and unlike the Airflow, the Airstream featured a convertible in the line-up. The Airflow was never available in convertible form because the top-down position would have compromised the aerodynamic and structural properties of its design. DeSoto dealers who still had 1934 Airflows on the lot were able to obtain retro kits that gave the 1934 models an updated 1935 appearance. Chrysler also sold the Airflow design in England as the Chrysler Croydon.

For 1936, DeSoto offered both the Series S-2 Airflow and S-1 Airstream cars, but the writing was on the wall for the third edition of the Airflow models. While the Airflow was only available in coupe or sedan style, the Airstream featured a multitude of body styles available in both the DeLuxe and Custom line. Styling for the Airstream was also enhanced by the fact that famed designer Ray Dietrich was now Chief of Design for the Chrysler Corporation, and his input gave the Airstream a touch of class. Bolstered by the new Airstream, sales of DeSoto increased a whopping 54 percent, but this was not due to the Airflow, of which only 5,000 were built. The king of the Chrysler camp was still the low-priced Plymouth, as the

Thanks Mr. Zeder–

FOR THESE RIDE IMPROVEMENTS

Elbow rests tailored to conform to your arm. Comfortably padded, and so shaped that they add greater width to De Soto's exceptionally wide rear seat. The arm rest is fitted with ash receiver.

More and thinner leaves in the rear springs, made possible by a new spring material called "Amola" steel . . . made still more resilient by *tapering* at the ends of the leaves. This eliminates at the very source the cause of squeaks. In addition they are equipped with metal covers protecting them against the weather.

Shock absorbers of a new, improved type make riding smoother than ever. Their purpose is to arrest movement after the springs have absorbed the shock of the bump. And the Ride Stabilizer prevents lurching and side-sway when the car is rounding a curve or passing another car.

Rear Seats conform to body. Greater depth has been added to De Soto's already exceptionally wide rear seat. And all seats are higher . . . "chair height" . . . coming up under and supporting the knees for easier riding.

Individual (knee-type) front wheel springs, as developed by Chrysler Corporation engineers . . . have proved soundest by millions of miles in actual use. In all this time, to our knowledge, not one single spring has been broken. Synchronized with the rear leaf springs, they add materially to De Soto's smooth Floating Ride.

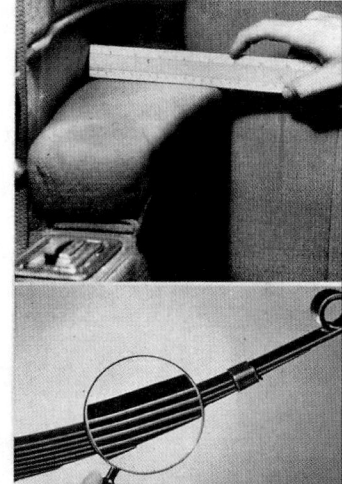

THIS IS FRED ZEDER, Vice-chairman of the Board, in charge of engineering of the Chrysler Corp., whose mission in life is to take the bumps out of the lives of others . . . particularly out of the lives of De Soto owners.

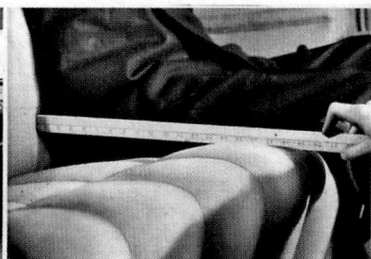
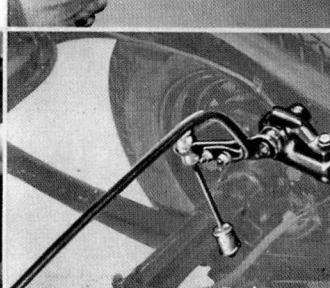

Fred Zeder, Chrysler's Vice-Chairman of the Board for Engineering, was featured in this 1936 DeSoto brochure taking credit for DeSoto's smooth ride. *From the Les Pesavento Collection*

motoring public found favor in its price and reliability. Rival Ford suffered severe losses for 1936, and the number one position would go to Chevrolet. DeSoto ranked 13th for the year, but the forecast was good. DeSotos were still being manufactured at the Chrysler plant, but ground was broken for a new facility in Detroit that would be exclusively dedicated to DeSoto production. This plant would begin turning out cars in 1937, and for the first time in its eight-year history, DeSotos were now built on an assembly line of their own.

Only one series was offered for 1937, and it was known as the S-3. With the Airflow no longer in the line-up, DeSoto could now concentrate its resources on building a car for all needs. Available in no less than 10 different body styles, the S-3 was a handsome car that clearly displayed the talented efforts of Ray Dietrich. A sleek and stylish convertible was available for $975, and a three-passenger business coupe could be had for as little as $770. A DeSoto Suburban was also available this year, but it was not a factory offering. Instead, DeSoto shipped a standard 116-inch wheelbase S-3 chassis to J. C. Cantrell & Company in Huntington, Long Island, New York, for fitting out as a wood-bodied wagon. This was a one-year-only offering, but the Suburban name would resurface after World War II in the S-11 model. There was also an emphasis on safety that year, and a restyled interior in the S-3 fea-

Selling for $1,300, the 1937 Series S-3 Convertible Sedan was the most expensive DeSoto for the year, and only 426 were built. *From the Les Pesavento Collection*

tured recessed instrument panel knobs, flush-mounted gauges, and a speedometer mounted directly in front of the steering column. The S-3 helped DeSoto move up to rank 11th for U.S. automobiles. A grand total of 86,541 cars were built for the calendar year.

With war clouds gathering over Europe, the U.S. auto market found itself in a slump for 1938. The recession was also attributed to the need for a balance in the market following several years of recovery from the Great Depression. All of the major manufacturers felt its icy grip, but DeSoto still managed to

give the S-3 a face-lift and call it the new S-5. Advertised under the slogan, "America's Smartest Low-Priced Car" the Ray Dietrich styling treatment clearly defined the handsome profile of the S-5. Wheelbases were increased, refinements were made to the trusty L-Head Six that included an optional aluminum cylinder head that increased horsepower to an even 100, and a new chassis featured independent front wheel suspension and semi-elliptic leaf rear springs. The headlights also began sinking down into the front fenders on the S-5, and the following year they would be mounted within the

BUILT TO WITHSTAND shock and twisting strain, De Soto's new chassis is stronger, more rigid. Frame side rails are 6 inches deep, with improved X-member. New strong sub side-rails contribute to safety.

For 1938, DeSoto offered a new chassis design that featured an improved X-member and six-inch-deep side-rails. *From the Les Pesavento Collection*

fenders themselves. As with the S-3, the S-5 also featured a one-piece windshield, a styling feature that would disappear on DeSotos the following year and would not reappear until a new one-piece curved windshield was introduced on the 1953 models.

The S-3 was actually the beginning of the S-Series model designation that would carry the company all the way through 1957 with the S-27. A study of the S-Series clearly defines the year-over-year refinements of the American automobile. The S-3 and S-5 styles laid the foundation for the refinement of styling in DeSoto that now enlisted the input of sales people and consumers. DeSotos for 1939 were the result of a market survey from Ray Dietrich's department; and dealers as well as prospective car buyers were questioned regarding all aspects of what they wanted in an automobile. The result was a redesigned DeSoto for 1939 known as the S-6. The DeSoto was now becoming a car of beauty as well as a reliable

means of transportation. Smooth, sweeping lines, headlights housed completely within the front fenders, a two-piece "V" windshield, and a gentle curve on the lower body line suggested running boards were soon going to disappear. DeSoto offered no convertible in the S-6 Series, but an option called the Sedan Skylight featured a sunroof. The skylight feature did not prove to be very popular and was dropped as an option with little fanfare. The S-6 also was available in two trim levels; the DeLuxe and Custom, with the Custom line featuring a bit more refinement in its trim appointments than the DeLuxe.

The year 1940 found the U.S. automobile industry changing as war clouds in Europe were raining down hard. In time, all of Detroit's car builders would see their fair share of war production contracts, but for now there was still room for passenger car production. Two events in 1940 affected the Chrysler Corporation profoundly. The first was an eight-

The smart looking DeSoto coupe rode on a 119-inch wheelbase and sold for just $870. *From the Les Pesaven-to Collection*

week strike that stalled production late in 1939, and thus delayed all of Chrysler's new products for 1940. The second occurred on August 18, 1940, when Walter P. Chrysler passed away. From his humble beginnings in Ellis, Kansas, to one of the giants of the automotive industry, Chrysler had certainly made his mark in the world, and his presence at the Chrysler Corporation would surely be missed.

Despite the loss of Walter Chrysler, and the devastating strike, DeSoto introduced the gorgeous S-7. Streamlining was the watchword for the new S-7, as it was found in many of its design features. This was an all-new DeSoto that had a new body and featured a better ride, thanks to the redistribution of weight by moving the seats and engine forward in the frame. DeSoto continued its famous "Floating Power," and there were still two series offered with defi-

nite trim appointments dividing the DeLuxe from the Custom. Ads in DeSoto's brochures for 1940 proudly proclaimed, "Look—the Back's as Beautiful as the Front!" DeSoto also touted "Safety-Signal Instruments," which featured a speedometer that changed colors as speeds increased. The S-7 even featured a 7-passenger sedan limousine that sold for $1,290. This was very costly for the mid-priced DeSoto, and only 34 were built.

The U.S. automobile business was humming along in 1941, but anyone who read a newspaper or listened to the radio knew that war was on the horizon. Although production of automobiles would continue through the year without restrictions, the industry also managed to crank out an astounding amount of war goods as well. Not to be left behind, DeSoto jumped into the patriotic fever sweeping the nation and began manufacturing small items at first, but then moved onto bigger parts and contracts. The Chrysler Corporation built airplane wings, fuselages, engines, guns, and tanks for the war effort. Although war manufacturing was stepping up in 1941, DeSoto still managed to offer the S-8. Billed as an "All-new car," the S-8 still used the tried and proven L-Head Six with a few modifications made for more power. The most notable change for the new DeSoto in 1941 was its bold front-end treatment, which featured a waterfall theme that DeSoto would refine and use on several models. The year 1941 also marked DeSoto's introduction of the Simplimatic transmission that was connected to the engine via a "Fluid Drive" coupling. The Fluid Drive coupling was revolutionary right from the start, and introduced the motoring public to the concept of driving without having to shift gears. Shifting was automatic, and the Chrysler Corporation was on its way to making driving a more pleasurable experience for everyone.

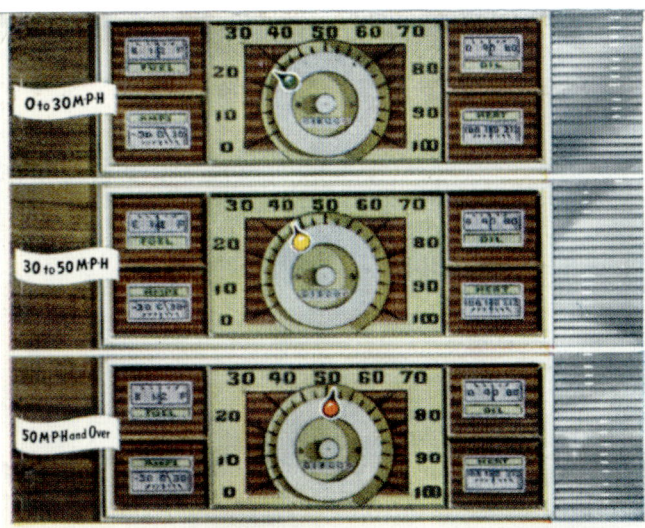

NEW SAFETY-SIGNAL Speedometer . . . the most ingenious ever put on a car! An electric "eye" shows green, amber, red to advise you of your safe driving speed range.

A new safety feature for 1939 was the Safety-Signal Speedometer. The pointer actually changed colors as speeds progressed. *From the Les Pesavento Collection*

DeSoto crossed into the 1940s with the even more streamlined S-7, which was available in Custom or DeLuxe trim. In this artist's rendering from the 1940 brochure, a seven-passenger sedan races by the airport. *From the Les Pesavento Collection*

For 1940, Chrysler's export division featured a line of trucks for every purpose. Pick-ups, tankers, stake bodies, dumps, and even a school bus were available under the DeSoto name. *From the Les Pesavento Collection*

Sales of the S-8 were acceptable for 1941, but it placed last in the Chrysler camp with Plymouth, Dodge, and Chrysler all outselling DeSoto. DeSoto was ranked 10th in model year production with 99,999 DeLuxe and Custom models leaving the factory. (One has to wonder why they didn't build just one more for an even 100,000 units.) Versatility was again DeSoto's strong point as a multitude of body styles were offered in both lines. Sedans, coupes, convertibles, long wheelbase sedans, and even a Sky-View taxi was offered that featured a sunroof above the passenger compartment—presum-

ably for looking up at those wonderful new skyscrapers in the cities of America. The year 1941 would turn out to be the last full year of production before the U.S. entered World War II. Restrictions on materials needed for building cars began to have an impact on production, and 1942 would turn out to be an abbreviated year for all car builders.

Both DeSoto and its cousin Plymouth began producing the 1942 models as quickly as possible, since the impending shutdown of U.S. automobile production was looming. DeSoto now offered the S-10S and the S-10C Series,

Front wing windows serve as wind breakers for driver and front seat passengers.

A full-width rear seat. Big enough for three. plenty of leg room.

Note particularly the special rear window which improves visibility for rear seat passengers and helps control ventilation.

Sketch of DeSoto Convertible Club Coupe

it is as gay and carefree as all "outdoors" yet makes a perfect year-round car. The trim-tailored top is power-operated. goes up or down automatically.

For 1941, DeSoto offered the Series S-8, and this Convertible Club Coupe sold for $1,195 at introduction. DeSoto raised prices and the same model sold for $1,240 by the middle of the year. *From the Les Pesavento Collection*

also known as the DeLuxe and Custom, respectively, late in the summer of 1941. With war clouds hovering, business was good. In what was perhaps one of the boldest styling statements made in 1942, DeSoto featured a front-end that was again redesigned and featured hidden headlamps. The retractable doors that concealed the headlamps were mechanically operated, and a pull-type handle much like an emergency brake opened the doors. With the headlamp doors closed, the front-end of the S-10 was sleek and smooth. The S-10's waterfall styled grille was expanded and DeSoto now had a very distinctive nose that made it recognizable from any distance. Unfortunately, the hidden headlamp treatment would only appear on the S-10, for after the war DeSoto's headlights would once again be exposed.

In accordance with government orders, DeSoto ceased production on February 9, 1942. One can only speculate as to what total production of the S-10 might have been if production was not cut short, but lady liberty was calling and America now had a new focus. The United States of America needed help, and DeSoto stood ready to deliver. Indeed, DeSoto was going to war.

Featuring a cavernous rear trunk compartment, the Custom Coupe for 1941 was a favorite with traveling salesmen of the day. The huge trunk could hold everything from machine parts to cartons of cigarettes. *From the Les Pesavento Collection*

1942 DE SOTO

. . . Chrysler Corporation's Style Leader

For 1942, DeSoto was on the cutting edge of style as the Series S-10 featured "Airfoil" headlamps that were out-of-sight when closed. It was a beautiful design that would not return in the postwar S-11. *From the Les Pesavento Collection*

The streamlined styling of the S-10 made for an attractive car with its unique front end design. Power came from the trusty 236.7 cubic-inch L-Head Six rated at 115 horsepower. *Artwork by John Satterthwaite*

SPECIAL

Fifth Avenue ENSEMBLE

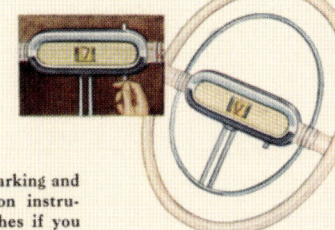

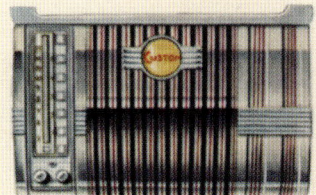

A special option package was offered on the S-10 that made it a luxurious car. Note the cigarette dispenser mounted in the steering wheel hub; a very rare option in the present-day collector market. *From the Les Pesavento Collection*

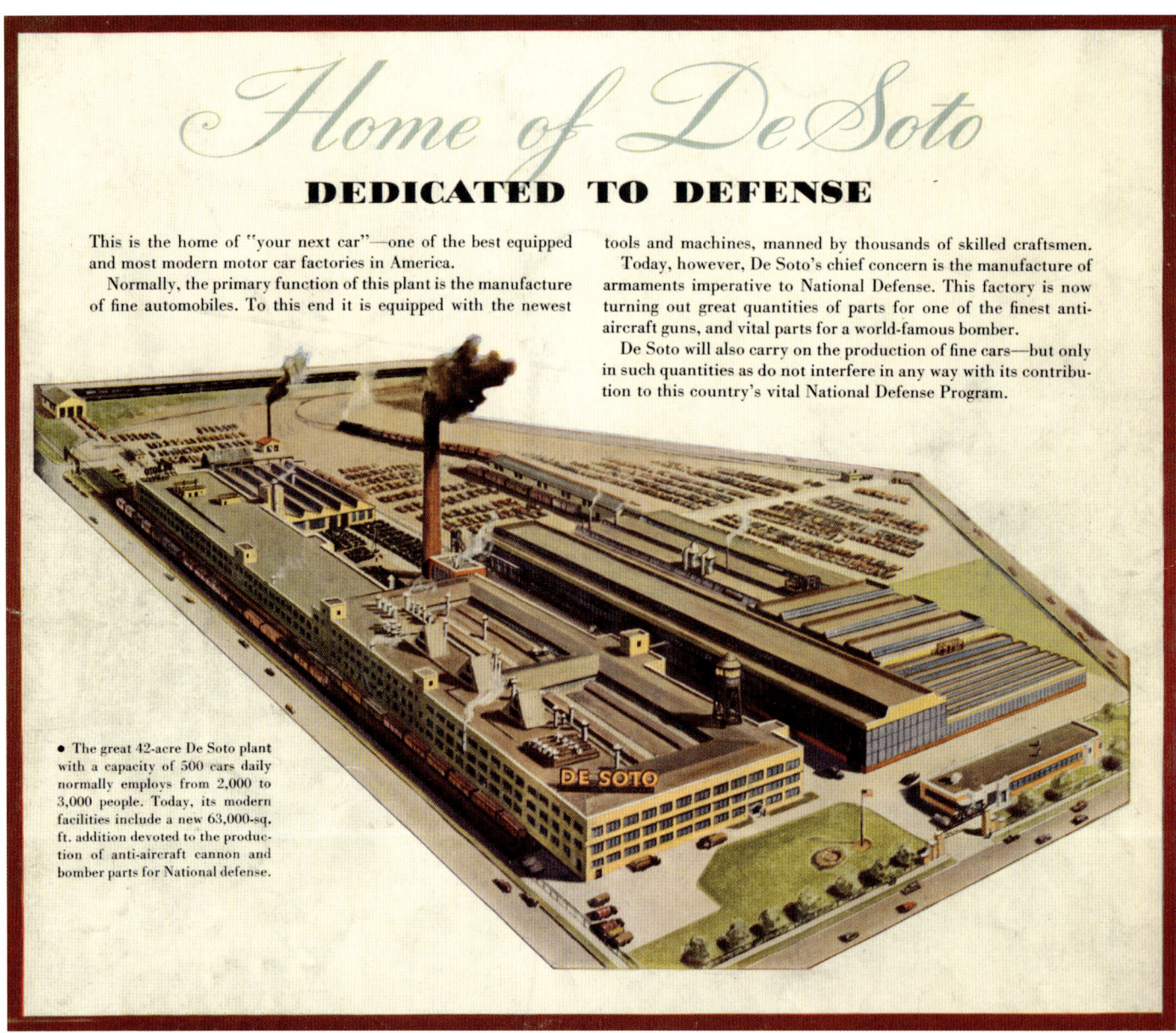

Home of DeSoto
DEDICATED TO DEFENSE

This is the home of "your next car"—one of the best equipped and most modern motor car factories in America.

Normally, the primary function of this plant is the manufacture of fine automobiles. To this end it is equipped with the newest tools and machines, manned by thousands of skilled craftsmen.

Today, however, De Soto's chief concern is the manufacture of armaments imperative to National Defense. This factory is now turning out great quantities of parts for one of the finest anti-aircraft guns, and vital parts for a world-famous bomber.

De Soto will also carry on the production of fine cars—but only in such quantities as do not interfere in any way with its contribution to this country's vital National Defense Program.

● The great 42-acre De Soto plant with a capacity of 500 cars daily normally employs from 2,000 to 3,000 people. Today, its modern facilities include a new 63,000-sq. ft. addition devoted to the production of anti-aircraft cannon and bomber parts for National defense.

DeSoto's brochure for 1942 featured an artist's rendering of the factory, and proudly lamented the fact that it was more than ready for production of war goods. *From the Les Pesavento Collection*

PRODUCTS OF CHRYSLER CORPORATION
ARMY TANKS · ANTI-AIRCRAFT GUNS · AIRCRAFT PARTS · ARMY VEHICLES
PASSENGER CARS · TRUCKS · MARINE AND INDUSTRIAL ENGINES · DIESEL
ENGINES · OILITE BEARINGS · AIRTEMP HEATING AND AIR CONDITIONING

DeSoto was not attempting to hide its war efforts in advertising for 1942. DeSoto, as well as the entire Chrysler Corporation, would go on to contribute fighting machines of all shapes and sizes. *From the Les Pesavento Collection*

Chapter 4

WAR AND PEACE

The war clouds that had enveloped Europe finally reached America on December 7, 1941. While the attack on Pearl Harbor caught the sleeping island off guard, the automobile industry was already prepared. Indeed, U.S. car companies had already begun to "tool up" for the war effort several years before, and the full-scale manufacturing of war goods forced production of DeSoto's S-10 to be cut short. All civilian automobile production ceased on February 9, 1942, and only 24,771 S-10s were manufactured, with a mere 4,186 built in the calendar year 1942. War production was clearly taking over as America entered the conflict on two fronts. The Chrysler Corporation already had contracts from the U.S. government in place when car production ceased, so the step up to full-scale manufacture of war goods was the next logical progression. Many of Chrysler's tooling and plant fixtures were easily adaptable to producing badly needed parts for war machines. The M4 Sherman tank used parts from Chrysler, Plymouth, and DeSoto, and the 66,500-pound armor-plated warrior was the backbone of the U.S. Army's offensive capabilities. Chrysler even created a monster engine for the M4A4 tank by combining five of its six-cylinder engines to create a 30-cyl-

inder behemoth that generated an astounding 425 horsepower. Chrysler and GM's Cadillac division would go on to become the nation's largest builders of tanks for the war effort. The Plymouth division immediately went to work on the Bofors anti-aircraft gun. These

A bust of Hernando de Soto graced the hood of DeSoto's Series S-14 automobiles for 1950. *Artwork by John Satterthwaite*

WING SECTIONS BY DeSoto

"WING SECTIONS BY DE SOTO" is the title of another chapter in the war production story told by De Soto plants and craftsmen —and retold on the battle fronts as the products of De Soto go into action.

These wing section jobs by De Soto also call for faultless workmanship — in keeping with the critical task they must perform when they become the means of flight for combat airplanes.

De Soto has gone far afield, indeed, since the days of its fine motor car production. The remotest theatres of war are, today, the scene of DeSoto action, as the basic parts of artillery, aircraft and combat vehicles carry on the De Soto tradition of precision manufacture—on sea, land, and in the air.

Here, at home, the De Soto service sign is more than ever a symbol of courtesy and efficiency. With ample parts and skillful service, De Soto dealers are doing a fine job for their owners today.

DE SOTO WAR PRODUCTION includes the precision building of airplane wing sections— bomber fuselage nose and center sections—vital assemblies for anti-aircraft guns and General Sherman Tanks—and a variety of manufacturing services to American war industry.

· · ·

War Bonds—Your Personal Investment in Victory

DE SOTO DIVISION OF CHRYSLER CORPORATION

TUNE IN ON MAJOR BOWES, EVERY THURSDAY, 9:00 TO 9:30 P. M., EASTERN WAR TIME

An ad from 1944 proudly displays DeSoto's contribution to the war effort. DeSoto built wing sections for this Curtiss SB2C-1 Helldiver. *Society of Automotive Historians, Dunwoodie Archives/AACA Library and Research Center*

Vital De Soto Transportation

Airplane photos courtesy American Airlines, Inc.

Regular inspections and service operations mean safe and reliable transport by our nation's airlines. Here, a big airplane engine gets its daily inspection.

Periodic inspections by trained mechanics of De Soto dealers help De Sotos and Plymouths to run efficiently. Above, a De Soto is getting its Spring Tune-up.

The great airliners are constantly serviced. Each day they're given rigid and careful inspections. At regular intervals, all planes are completely overhauled.

Here, expert help lubricates and inspects a war working De Soto. Large repairs are often prevented by small adjustments made during these inspections.

Every airport's a service station for the airliners. The airlines' great record of dependable travel is a high tribute to rigid inspection and service schedules.

Backed by their dealers, De Sotos are delivering superior transportation. Upkeep is low. Tire mileage—high. De Soto comfort—a special, *extra* value to owners.

THERE'S a striking parallel these days between your fine De Soto and the great airliners. Both were carefully built for lasting, efficient transportation. Both are turning in brilliant wartime records. Both deliver top performances when serviced regularly.

Today, despite wartime restrictions of new equipment, airlines are setting a magnificent record for dependable travel through the regular inspection and service of equipment.

So, you proud De Soto owners, take a tip from the airlines. Insure maximum efficiency of your wartime De Soto by having regular check-ups. Your De Soto dealer has expert help for whatever work is necessary. He has factory-engineered replacement parts. And he's delivering war-winning service. He's ready to help keep your De Soto running in top condition—through Victory.

★

DE SOTO DIVISION OF CHRYSLER CORPORATION

★

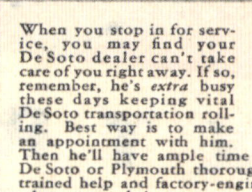
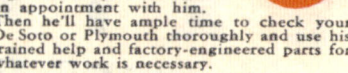

When you stop in for service, you may find your De Soto dealer can't take care of you right away. If so, remember, he's *extra* busy these days keeping vital De Soto transportation rolling. Best way is to make an appointment with him. Then he'll have ample time to check your De Soto or Plymouth thoroughly and use his trained help and factory-engineered parts for whatever work is necessary.

DE SOTO WAR PRODUCTION includes the precision building of airplane wing sections—bomber fuselage nose and center sections—vital assemblies for anti-aircraft guns and General Sherman Tanks—and a variety of special manufacturing services to American war industry.

TUNE IN ON MAJOR BOWES EVERY THURSDAY, CBS, 9 P.M., E.W.T.

LET'S ALL BACK THE ATTACK—BUY MORE WAR BONDS

This ad encouraged DeSoto owners to perform regular maintenance on the DeSoto in order to get through the war. The ad likens the maintenance of an airliner to that of an automobile. *Society of Automotive Historians, Dunwoodie Archives/AACA Library and Research Center*

guns were fairly versatile in their use, as they could be mounted on wheels or turrets. The original design for the Bofors gun was of Swedish origin, but there were no provisions for its mass production. Stepping up production of the Bofors gun required a new assembly plant, which was one of many facility expansion programs going on at Chrysler for the war effort. The Bofors 40-mm gun was used on the decks of America's greatest battleships including the U.S.S. *Missouri*, the U.S.S *Iowa*, and the U.S.S. *Massachusetts*. When fired in pairs the sounds from the 40-mm barrels made for an impressive volley of firepower.

Not to be left out, DeSoto began building nose and center fuselage sections for the Martin B-26 Marauder. The Marauder was a medium-sized bomber whose primary task was close tactical ground support, and it saw action in the Pacific and Mediterranean Theaters. With knowledge gained from work on the Marauder, DeSoto went on to build sections of the famous B-29 Superfortress. With a wingspan of 141.3 feet, the B-29 was America's biggest bomber ever built for the Air Force, and DeSoto landed the contract for building the nose section. The nose section for the B-29 was a difficult manufacturing endeavor owing to the

An ad from the August 1943 edition of *American Home* touts the fact that women were an intricate part of the war effort. The Chrysler Corporation employed over 20,000 women during the war. *From the Dennis David Collection*

fact that its flight controls were complicated, and it was also capable of being pressurized for high-altitude flying. Other contributions to the war effort from DeSoto were the wing sections for the Curtiss SB2C-1 Helldiver, which was one of the primary planes used for offensive strikes over Japan. All of this manufacturing

Built by the Chrysler Corporation, this massive 30-cylinder tank engine cranked out over 400 horsepower. It was built by mating five six-cylinder engines together. *Courtesy of the Chrysler Museum, Auburn Hills, Michigan. Photo by Les Pesavento*

at DeSoto's production plant took place with the help of parts from Chrysler, Dodge, and Plymouth, and the entire company put forth an incredible effort toward winning the war.

When it was all over, DeSoto found itself in the same position as all other U.S. car builders. The motoring public wanted new cars, but material shortages and labor problems would make returning to civilian automobile production difficult for the entire industry. The post-World War II market for U.S. automobiles was a time like no other. Returning GIs had dollars to spend, but Detroit had to make the monumental switch over to building cars after the most extensive industrial retooling effort in history. This created an unbalanced market

that did not favor consumers, and it would be several years before a "buyers" market would return.

DeSoto's first postwar offering came in the form of the S-11S and the S-11C, more commonly known as the lower line DeLuxe and the upper line Custom, respectively. Although they rode on the same 121.5- and 139.5-inch prewar wheelbases, they were restyled just enough to let the general public know that something new was going on. These were truly beautiful cars with their front fenders swept back into the doors, rear fenders that almost gave the impression of fender skirts, and wraparound bumpers. The S-11 would find favor with many commercial vehicle companies as

Of all the De Soto cars ever built, 7 out of 10 are still running

Thousands upon thousands of motorists have been happily wedded to De Soto for years! Wedded to cars that are now rolling up 100,000 miles...200,000 miles...even more. You see, our engineers decided 17 years ago *to make and keep making a better car.* Which accounts for the many notable features they've given it...things like floating power, fluid drive, superfinished parts, safety-steel bodies. Today, De Soto manufacturing skill is going into bomber sections, airplane wings, guns. But look forward to the day when we'll again be making De Soto cars for you...cars *designed to endure.*

DE SOTO DIVISION, CHRYSLER CORPORATION

Tune in Chrysler Corporation's program, "Music of Morton Gould," Thursdays, 9 P. M., E. W. T.

BACK THE ATTACK — BUY MORE WAR BONDS THAN BEFORE

DeSoto
DESIGNED TO ENDURE

DeSoto regularly placed ads exploiting the longevity of their cars during the war effort. In this artist's rendering, a prewar S-10 is handling wedding duty during the war. *From the Dennis David Collection*

In this advertisement, published during a time when doctors still made house calls, an S-10 awaits its call to duty during a storm. *From the Dennis David Collection*

With the war finally over, the Chrysler Corporation touted the smooth ride of its family of fine cars. This ad shows a young lady holding her fish bowl while under way in a Plymouth. *From the Dennis David Collection*

a taxi. Indeed, DeSoto taxis could be seen in just about any major metropolitan city in the immediate postwar era. With roomy interiors and excellent reliability, the S-11 promised good service for a number of years while traversing America's city streets. Tooling for the S-11's bumper was simplified, as it was interchangeable between the front and rear with the rear usually embossed with *Fluid Drive* written directly in the center. The waterfall grille was continued and was now spread across the entire length of the front end. A close look at the S-11's grille clearly demonstrates its relation to the prewar S-10 model. One styling feature that did not make it into the postwar S-11 was the S-10's hidden headlamps. The S-11 also clearly demonstrated that running boards

were going the way of the dinosaur, and they would disappear altogether after 1949. Most of the cars in Chrysler's postwar line-up featured sweeping front fenders running into the doors. But the lone holdout was Plymouth, which still had its fenders cut short at the cowl. Plymouth would not receive the sweeping front fender treatment until it caught up with the rest of the Chrysler camp in 1949.

DeSoto also continued to service its export market after the war with the DeSoto Diplomat. For 1946, DeSoto dealers outside North America offered a Diplomat based on Plymouth's P-15 Series. The car was essentially a Plymouth with right-hand drive, DeSoto badges, medallions, hubcaps, and a modified DeSoto grille. Originally introduced in 1938,

DeSoto's first postwar car came in the form of the S-11, which would stay in production with only minor changes until early 1949. This model is a 1948 S-11 Custom Club Coupe. *Photo by Dennis David*

the Diplomat met the needs of foreign markets, and it used a Plymouth-based format. In many instances, foreign governments wanted a different DeSoto than the American version sold in their market in order to stop the illegal importation of automobiles. The DeSoto Diplomat also used the best of both worlds, as the smaller Plymouth was better suited for narrower roads and the name recognition of Hernado de Soto, the great explorer, was more familiar to many local populations. The Diplomat name would eventually go on to outlive DeSoto itself after 1961, as a DeSoto Diplomat was offered for a short time in South Africa after 1963.

The DeSoto S-11 Series would stay around for a full three years and even dip into 1949,

being introduced as a first series 1949 model on December 1, 1948. Although DeSoto had long changed its model year production back in 1931 to a January to December accounting method, problems in getting automobile production up and running again mandated that the S-11 be continued unchanged into 1949. There was no new model introduction or banners announcing the event; instead the S-11 model quietly assumed 1949 status until a second series made its debut in March. Known as the S-13, the DeSoto was now shedding its rounded lines of the 1940s and moving into the 1950s. While other carmakers were beginning to look to the future of automotive styling with their longer, lower, and wider cars, Chrysler's products still held a conservative approach that

A graceful flying goddess adorned the hood of the S-11. The goddess was also available in a luminescent plastic with a light underneath it that lit up with the headlights. *Photo by Dennis David*

implied practicality over style. This was due mostly to Chrysler's President K. T. Keller, who thought that the American automobile was moving toward a design of impracticality. Of course, the new S-13 made good sense; it was tall and roomy, and you could even wear your hat in it while driving, but its proportions did not lend itself well to the changing look of the U.S. automobile. The S-13 did well for DeSoto with 95,051 cars built during the model year. The postwar car demand was still strong, and DeSoto still had a strong foothold in the market, but all this would change over the course of the next decade.

As America entered the "Decade of Innocence" it did so with a robust year for the American automobile industry. Sales of U.S. automobiles for 1950 were even better than in

1949, but the market was now getting saturated and the next few years would see the demise of several independent car builders. After being the first out of the starting gate with an all-new postwar car, Kaiser introduced the new Series K512 model for 1951. But Kaiser would not see the end of the decade, as it became another casualty of the U.S. automobile industry in 1955. Indeed, before the decade was over Packard, Nash, and Hudson would also close their doors, leaving the majority of production of U.S. cars to General Motors, Ford, and Chrysler.

DeSoto entered 1950 with the new S-14 model, again available in the DeLuxe and Custom version, and literally unchanged from the previous year. A latecomer in 1950 was a new, all-steel-bodied six-passenger station wagon. It

Perhaps one of the ultimate family cars ever built, the S-11 Suburban had enough room to carry the family or a traveling band. It rode on a 139.5-inch wheelbase. *From the Les Pesavento Collection*

would go on to replace the traditional wood bodied wagon, which was in its last year. DeSoto had a long history of enlisting the help of celebrities with sales, and this year Groucho Marx stepped up to tout the new DeSoto with a series of radio and television shows. Strangely enough, DeSoto's advertising was also centered on an ad slogan that proudly proclaimed "The New DeSoto" but only minor styling upgrades made it distinguishable from its predecessor. A retooled rear fender, larger rear window, and the continued refinement of the DeSoto's trademark grille were all that was new for the

S-14. DeSoto's trusty Powermaster L-Head six-cylinder engine was also unchanged. Soldiering on with several major refinements over the years, DeSoto's L-Head Six now developed 112 horsepower and still featured the "Floating Power" mounting for vibration dampening. While the DeSoto for the new decade was hardly anything new, the seed of change was planted, as K. T. Keller became chairman of the board of Chrysler. The presidency was assumed by Lester Colbert, who would initiate a change in direction that would keep Chrysler's products on par with the rest of the industry.

The S-11 Convertible was a beautiful car with its top down. This 1947 Custom S-11 sold new for $1,761. *Photo by Dennis David/2005 National DeSoto Convention-St Catherine's Ontario, Canada*

That change, however, would not come about until 1955 with the influence of Virgil Exner's "Forward Look."

For 1950, the Chrysler Corporation also marketed a line of trucks that carried the DeSoto name. First offered in 1938, DeSoto trucks were on their way to building a solid reputation throughout the world. The 1950 models were built on Dodge chassis, and used the alpha designations of F, G, and H. A cab-

over design was also marketed as the Series GM and HM. DeSoto had a truck for every purpose from small parcel deliveries to tractors capable of hauling heavy trailers. The foreign passenger car market also again featured the Diplomat in several body styles and they were distinguished from their American counterparts by a few trim changes. In the automobile market, DeSoto even offered a few body styles that were not available in the U.S. market, as

A 1952 MGM movie called "Talk About a Stranger" featured a sinister looking S-11 Convertible. The movie starred George Murphy. *From the Doug Dressler Collection*

a 2-door wagon and three-window Business coupe carried the Diplomat name.

For 1951, DeSoto did not completely retool a new car, but rather made do with a warmed over model from the previous year. Now known as the S-15-1 in the DeLuxe line, and the S-15-2 in the Custom line, these cars were built with another war cloud hanging overhead. The threat of hostilities in Korea caused the U.S. government to mandate restrictions on many materials, and the auto industry felt the shortage of supplies. For 1951, DeSotos were void of much of the brightwork that they were usually known for. DeSoto's waterfall grille was now replaced with a toothy unit that looked like it would need a dentist for a tune-up. This same grille would go on to become a favorite of hot rodders in the coming years. The all-steel wagon had taken over as the only wagon model offered, and was available in the Custom line only. It was a 4-door that featured a fold down rear seat for carrying cargo. The most expensive car in DeSoto's line-up was the long wheelbase nine-passenger Suburban, which sold for $3,566.

Due to the impending government restrictions on materials needed for building cars,

DeSoto introduced the S-13 in 1949. It was available in two trim levels as the DeLuxe and Custom. *From the Les Pesavento Collection*

A proud little boy poses near his dad's 1950 DeSoto Custom Sedan in suburban America. *From the Les Pesavento Collection*

DeSoto missed the window for development of a new model for 1952. The Korean War had put the Chrysler Corporation back to work on the war effort. Dodge built army trucks, Chrysler built its famous tank engines, Plymouth built air/seaplane hulls, and DeSoto built afterburners for the Pratt & Whitney J-48 Turbojet Wasp engine that powered the F-94 Starfire. All of this activity left little time and resources to build an all-new DeSoto, and the S-15 Series cars continued into 1952 with little change. There was, however, one big announcement when DeSoto introduced a new V-8 in February. The trusty L-Head Six was still available in the DeLuxe and Custom Series, but the new 276-cubic-inch V-8 was reserved for a line of its own known as the S-17 FireDome 8. This was DeSoto's first 8-cylinder car since the Model CF Eight back in 1931. The new FireDome 8 featured hemispherical combustion chambers that Chrysler's engineers claimed had a number of advantages over the standard technology of the day. The Chrysler

For 1951, DeSoto adopted a massive tooth-like front-end that featured nine molars up front. Due to the Korean War, production for 1951 and 1952 was counted as a single total. *From the Dennis David Collection*

Corporation was about to enter a new era of performance with several powerful engine options available in the DeSoto line-up. Styling for 1952 still featured a toothy grille up front, but was largely a carry-over design from the previous year. The shortage of raw materials created by the Korean War meant that there were very few resources left for a new design. A new aluminum two-barrel carburetor allowed DeSoto to lower the height of the hood slightly. This was also the era of DeSoto advertising with banners and flags covering practically every square inch of DeSoto showrooms everywhere. There was even a dome shaped "Fire-Dome Beanie" hat fitted with sparkplugs for salesmen to wear when touting the new Fire-Dome engine. Despite all of the promotion for the 1952 line-up, material and labor problems associated with the war and a nationwide steel strike made for a less than spectacular year for DeSoto, and it placed last in corporate sales

with just 97,585 built for the calendar year.

The export Diplomat for 1952 was again based on a Plymouth, but featured very little change from the previous year. A Custom-Special model featured a truly distinctive two-tone paint treatment that started at the roof and extended down through the rear trunk. The Diplomat was again offered in a multitude of body styles from wagons to convertibles. It is interesting to note that while the Diplomat was a DeSoto, the Chrysler Corporation counted it as a Plymouth with regard to internal accounting.

The DeLuxe and Custom names were eliminated for 1953, which was the 25th anniversary of DeSoto. (DeSoto was introduced in mid-1928 as a 1929 model.) In their place came the S-18 Series known as the Powermaster Six, and the FireDome V-8 known as the S-16 Series. The 25th anniversary of DeSoto occurred without a birthday cake, as there were

The big news for 1952 was V-8 power for DeSoto. The 276.1-cubic-inch engine developed 160 horsepower, and was available in the Series S-17 FireDome. In this factory photo workers are finishing off a line of V-8 engines. *From the Les Pesavento Collection*

The export DeSoto Diplomat was essentially a copy of the domestic Plymouth with a few minor differences. U.S. DeSotos carried 11 teeth while their foreign counterpart carried only seven. *From the Les Pesavento Collection*

no commemorative models or any publicity announcements marking the milestone. In theory, the lack of a celebration would appear to lend credence to the Chrysler Corporation's intent to discontinue DeSoto even at this early juncture. Evidence is found in Chrysler's pricing structure for 1953, which had a 2-door Club Coupe available from all divisions (except Imperial) with an odd pricing structure. A Plymouth Cambridge Club coupe could be had for a mere $1,707, a Dodge Meadowbrook for $1,958, and a Chrysler Windsor for $2,555. DeSoto's Club coupe in the Powermaster Six line sold for $2,434, just a mere $121 less than its Chrysler counterpart. The low, medium, and higher price structure is clearly seen in the numbers, but DeSoto seemed out of place somewhere in-between the middle and the top. Clearly there was something going on, and DeSoto would spend the next eight years

looking for a home in the Chrysler family.

Styling for 1953 was again a basic carryover from 1952, with just enough modifications made to give the public a different view. Front fenders now swept completely back to the rears, which now had a more integral look with the body. The long and sloping roofline was fitted with a full wraparound glass treatment that was seen the previous year on the FireDome 8 Sportsman. DeSoto also stepped into new territory with a foray into the dream car concept pioneered by Harley Earl. Introduced as the "Adventurer," it was designed by Virgil Exner and handcrafted by Ghia of Italy. Power came from a FireDome V-8, and the Adventurer spent 1954 on the show circuit touting DeSoto's vision of the future.

In a move to consolidate its operations, Chrysler purchased the Briggs Manufacturing Company in 1953. After purchasing most of their output for many years, the move served to cut Chrysler's costs in research and development for its new models. A milestone was reached at the Chrysler Corporation when Plymouth built its 8,000,000th car, a very respectable number for any company. The DeSoto was becoming a more refined automobile at this point. Amenities such as power brakes and air conditioning became available as options. America was entering the years of the great turnpike cruiser, and DeSoto would not be left behind in building some of these wonderful and comfortable automobiles.

For 1954, DeSoto again found itself little more than warmed-over in terms of styling. DeSoto's smiling grille featured teeth that

An early 1950s photo of the DeSoto plant on the corner of Wyoming and McGraw shows a multitude of different cars parked on the street. *From the Les Pesavento Collection*

The Distinguished
DeSoto
for 1953

DeSoto's grille for 1953 used 11 teeth. This is a FireDome V-8 Sedan. *From the Dennis David Collection*

were a little closer together than in the previous year, and it was clear that DeSoto was becoming the "odd-man-out" in the Chrysler family of cars. While these were wonderful cars offering reliability beyond compare, the fact is that they still had ties to the stodgy styling that K. T. Keller advocated back in 1949. Rivals General Motors and Ford had big plans in the works, and for 1955 both would com-

pletely restyle their cars thereby defining the 1950s automobile. DeSoto, in the mean time, still featured its top-heavy design that hardly advanced the company in the eyes of many motorists. The big news for the 1954 DeSoto was "Automatic," referring to several advances in drivability that made motoring a leisurely and pleasurable experience. The Powermaster Six was now designated the S-20, and the

Groucho Marx was enlisted to help promote the DeSoto line for 1954. An ornate showroom elegantly displays DeSoto's offerings. *From the Les Pesavento Collection*

FireDome V-8 was the S-19. The 1954 models received new grilles, new bumpers, and just enough new trim pieces to differentiate them from the previous year's models. There was also a major emphasis on interiors for 1954 with new colors keyed to exterior finishes. A special offering from DeSoto made its debut in 1954, and was called the Coronado. Harking back to the explorer image of Hernado himself, the Coronado was a 4-door sedan that featured its own fabulous colors of Cadiz Blue and Sahara Beige, and also featured two-tone interiors that were truly spectacular.

A new buzzword was taking hold in the Chrysler camp that would become a hallmark of design, as the "Forward Look" was coming into vogue. While the phrase had little to do with an actual styling exercise for 1954, it would be picked up and used extensively for the 1955 model year. Chrysler executives realized in 1954 that DeSoto's proposed designs for the 1955 model year had problems. They were certainly bound to be the trusty and reliable automobile that DeSoto had come to be known for, but when the Chrysler Corporation personnel got a sneak peak at what General Motors and Ford had in mind for 1955, they knew they were in trouble. The low and sleek Chevrolet Bel Air would clearly demonstrate the sensational styling of the 1950s, and Ford's new Fairlane Series featured a similar long and low look. Ford and Chevrolet were even offering the sporty Thunderbird and Corvette to lure customers to the showrooms. All this was going on while DeSoto still had plans for a tall and boxy looking car on the drawing boards. If DeSoto were to survive for 1955, it would take the efforts of a true genius to turn things around. That effort would come in the form of a man named Virgil Exner, who would take the "Forward Look" theme to new heights, and turn the once stodgy DeSoto into a new and advanced design.

DeSoto offered customers six- or eight-cylinder power for 1954, along with a multitude of body styles. This FireDome V-8 Sedan sold for $2,673. *Photo by Dennis David/2005 National DeSoto Convention-St Catherine's Ontario, Canada*

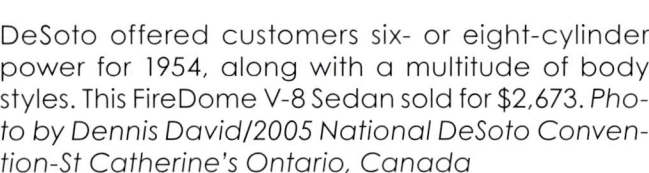

DeSoto introduced a dream car to the public in 1953 with the Adventurer; a sleek coupe designed by Virgil Exner and built by Ghia of Italy. The 170-horsepower FireDome V-8 powered it. *From the Les Pesavento Collection*

For 1954 another concept car called the Adventurer II wooed the crowds at the auto shows. Just as its predecessor, it too was powered by the FireDome V-8, which provided 170 horsepower. Only one was ever built. *From the Les Pesavento Collection*

The all-steel bodied FireDome V-8 wagon featured striking colors and a beautiful two-tone plaid interior. Formally known as the Series S-19, it sold for $3,361 and 946 were built. *From the Dennis David Collection*

Chapter 5

THE FORWARD LOOK

One look at DeSoto's design proposals for the 1955 model was all it took for Virgil Exner to realize that there could be big trouble on the horizon for the Chrysler Corporation. The U.S. economy was steaming ahead, and everything from toys to refrigerators was enjoying sales like no one had ever seen. Unless the Chrysler Corporation could find a quick fix for its 1955 line-up, it was in danger of becoming a non-player in the U.S. automobile market.

The answer came from within, as K. T. Keller had hired Virgil Exner back in 1949. Exner came to Chrysler as an experienced designer with many years of experience under his belt. He had previously worked for a firm called Advertising Artists, which had a contract with Studebaker. Exner honed his artistic skills doing illustration work for Studebaker models, which he did quite well. He then worked for General Motors at its Pontiac division before being hired away from GM to work directly for Studebaker, which resulted in his working with great designers like Bob Bourke, Ray Loewy, and Gordon Buehrig. When Raymond

Virgil Exner's new "Forward Look" styling gave DeSoto a whole new look for 1955. Both the Fireflite and the FireDome rode on 126-inch wheelbases and were attractive cars in two-tone paints. The Fireflite V-8 Sportsman seen here sold new for $2,939. *Photo by Dennis David/2005 National DeSoto convention- St. Catherines, Ontario Canada*

The Fireflite high-compression 291-cubic-inch V-8 generated 200 horsepower for 1955. *From the Dennis David Collection*

Loewy from Studebaker lured Exner away from General Motors, Harley Earl himself pleaded with Exner to stay on, but Virgil Exner saw an opportunity. He eventually started his own design studio and was responsible for the Studebaker Champion. A meeting in 1949 with K. T. Keller resulted in Exner going to work for Chrysler, and he would prove to be a critical factor in the Chrysler Corporation's success during the late 1950s. Exner would also go on to become Chrysler's vice president of design in 1957.

Exner had little time to spare when he was charged with reworking the 1955 line-up. In 1952, K. T. Keller asked him what he thought about the 1955 designs. Exner was less than enthusiastic. Keller then instructed Exner to redesign the 1955 line-up, which allowed only 18 months before tooling would commence

for the 1955 model year. This was not a lot of time, but Exner was up to the task. If the 1955 line-up was going to sell, the tall and boxy look that K. T. Keller had maintained for so long would have to go. Exner's talent would truly reveal itself in the new Forward Look for 1955. The new styles were an instant hit with all of Chrysler's divisions showing impressive gains. Chrysler had taken a chance and spent the handsome sum of $250 million on research and development. It had paid off and DeSoto was still a firm player in the game for 1955.

The Forward Look that Exner had devised literally took DeSoto several years ahead of the competition, and bodies were noticeably longer, wider, and lower for 1955. A panoramic wraparound windshield defined the Forward Look, and DeSoto still had its bright dental work up front with a seven-tooth grille that fea-

Factory photos of the 1955 Firedome Sportsman 4-door sedan clearly showed Virgil Exner's Forward Look styling theme. The new longer, wider, and lower appearance made for an attractive automobile. *From the Les Pesavento Collection*

tured floating parking lights. All 1955 DeSotos rode on a 126-inch wheelbase, and a plethora of bright and beautiful colors greeted buyers in the showrooms. Even more impressive was the all-new interior, which featured a futuristic "cockpit" design that was a direct concession to the aircraft-inspired designs of the day. Exner's design work for the 1955 DeSoto was a hit, and it would turn out to be a banner year.

DeSoto finally dropped the trustworthy six-cylinder engine in favor of V-8 power for all of its domestic production cars in 1955. The V-8 engine was actually built in two different power variations with the two-barrel version in the FireDome Series, which now had a lower case in the dome, and the four-barrel version in the new Fireflite Series. For 1955, the FireDome gained the S-22 Series

Anne Fogarty, famous fashion designer, drives a De Soto Sportsman.

DRIVE A [DE SOTO] BEFORE YOU DECIDE

There is no word in the English language that quite describes the utter satisfaction, the thrill, the delightful ease of driving a De Soto. Here is a car that translates your wishes into action almost with the speed of thought itself. There is an eager, natural response that is quite different from anything you're likely to find in other cars. That is why it is really important that you "drive a De Soto before you decide!" Your De Soto dealer will be delighted to have you take a turn at the wheel of either a Firedome or Fireflite. De Soto Division, Chrysler Corporation.

DE SOTO-PLYMOUTH dealers present **GROUCHO MARX** in "YOU BET YOUR LIFE" on NBC RADIO and TV

HOLIDAY/JUNE

A sharp 1955 DeSoto Sportsman is shown in a rear quarter shot with famous fashion designer Anne Fogarty behind the wheel. The bottom of the ad encourages prospective customers to tune into Groucho Marx's program called "You Bet Your Life." *From the Les Pesavento Collection*

Illustrator. Once design is "set," it is rendered in full color for careful study of various elements—over-all design, material texture, color harmony. Above Gloria Schaeffer completes this stage.

Long before the days of CAD computer design, illustrators used a pencil and paper to sketch new proposals. A DeSoto brochure from 1955 shows illustrator Gloria Schaeffer hard at work on an interior design. *From the Dennis David Collection*

designation, while the Fireflite was known as the S-21, and featured a fancy Coronado in the line-up. The Coronado for 1955 wore a tri-tone paint scheme and a luxurious leather interior that made it one of the ultimate cruisers of the 1950s. A new feature for 1955 was the unique dash-mounted shifter, which took the shifting mechanism out of the way of the driver's arms and legs. DeSoto brochures referred to the shifter as "Flite Control," and it was an impressive innovation in engineering design. The DeSoto FireDome and Fireflite models were cars that plied the nation's super highways with power and speed. Set apart from the competition by bright colors, powerful engines, and the unique Virgil Exner "Forward Look" styling theme, DeSoto had a great year in 1955 with a total of 115,485 cars being built for the model year.

DeSoto's Diplomat for 1955 was again based on a Plymouth chassis, and while the domestic DeSoto had seven teeth in its front grille, the Australian Diplomat had a grand total of 11 teeth. The Diplomat for 1955 was truly an homogenized automobile wearing pieces of both Plymouth and DeSoto. A different set of wheel covers, minor trim differences, and a few ornamental badges were all that differentiated the Diplomat from the standard Plymouth Belvedere. The Diplomat line also produced a 2-door station wagon for 1955,

The FireDome sedan for 1956 was available in a multitude of paint schemes. DeSoto would go on to sell 104,090 units for the calendar year. *Photo by Dennis David/2005 National DeSoto Convention-St Catherine's Ontario, Canada*

DeSoto paced the 33rd running of the Indianapolis 500. The pacing honors went to the Fireflite Convertible, as the top-of-the-line Adventurer was available only as a hardtop for 1956. In this photo, DeSoto President L. I. Woolson is at the wheel for the first test run. *From the Les Pesavento Collection*

but the 2-door wagon was still available. Although the domestic DeSoto had dropped the six-cylinder engine, it was still available in the Diplomat line-up. In 1955, Australia became its own market supplier when the U.S. tooling dies for the 1954 American-produced 4-door Diplomat sedans were sent there. This resulted in an Australian DeSoto that was unchanged for 1955. While all of the other markets continued to evolve, Australia's styling took a path all its own. An Australian model known as the UTE became very popular in 1956, and the Australian based DeSoto carried the 1954 styling all the way into 1957.

There was also a hint of styling excitement in the air for 1955, as Chrysler commissioned

A 1956 DeSoto Fireflite pace car convertible is a rare sight today. This one was photographed at the National DeSoto Convention in 2005. *Photo by Dennis David/2005 National DeSoto Convention-St Catherine's Ontario, Canada*

the building of three dream car concepts, with bodies by Ghia, on a DeSoto chassis. The first was a super looking roadster called the Falcon, which was designed by Chrysler's Advance Styling Studio. The Falcon featured a bold grid-type grille that was set far ahead of its recessed headlamps. The minimal use of chrome on the Falcon made for a tastefully conservative styling statement. Indeed, the major brightwork on the sides consisted of a set of exhaust side pipes and nothing else. Power for the Falcon came from a 1954 DeSoto V-8 rated at 170 horsepower, and its classic road-

Virgil Exner's "Forward Look" styling theme carried over into all aspects of DeSoto's design for 1956. Even this rear quarter panel trim piece on the 1956 pace car has a futuristic look. *Photo by Dennis David/2005 National DeSoto Convention-St Catherine's Ontario, Canada*

The Memphis Coach Company retrofitted the DeSoto Fireflite on a stretched wheelbase for 1956, making it the perfect car for airport or cab service. This car was available only through DeSoto's Fleet Sales office. *From the Doug Dressler Collection*

ster look made it a hit on the show circuit. In a hint of irony, Ford's Falcon would be the car that would break DeSoto's introductory sales record in 1960.

Also built for 1955 was the Flight Sweep I convertible, and Flight Sweep II hardtop. These cars showed the true vision of Virgil Exner, and shades of the all-new DeSoto for 1957 were glimpsed in the Flight Sweep dream cars. Built on a modified 1954 DeSoto chassis, both carried such wonderful features as hooded headlights, two-tone paint, sweeping bodylines, and prominent tailfins adorned the rear quarter panels. Wheel covers for the Flight

Sweeps even simulated an exposed brake drum shadowed by cooling fins. The Falcon, Flight Sweep I convertible, and the Flight Sweep II coupe wooed the crowds at the auto shows for the 1955 and 1956 seasons. Simply put, it was a great time to be a DeSoto, and while the general public may not have been able to put one of the glamorous dream cars in their driveways, they could drive home in a FireDome or Fireflite. DeSoto seemed as if it was on its way to true greatness in the coming years.

The mid-1950s was a wonderful time to be a child, and there were two themes that seemed to dominate the toys of the era. The first was

The Memphis Coach Company conversion of the DeSoto Fireflite made for ample room in the extended wheelbase sedan. *From the Doug Dressler Collection*

the American West, which featured cowboys and Indians constantly at odds with each other. The other theme was a growing infatuation with space. The United States and Russia were deep in the heart of the Cold War era, and the race for outer space would show up in many forms. For the U.S. automobile industry, a general growing trend in raising the height of the rear quarter panel would soon explode into the phenomenon known as the tailfin. The Italian carmaker Cisitalia had used the fin successfully on several of its racecars, and Harley Earl's design team had successfully introduced it on the 1948 Series 62 Cadillac. Virgil Exner's design

for Chrysler's 1956 products featured a unique tailfin that was tasteful and well proportioned to the overall body. DeSoto's line-up for 1956 featured this slight rise on the rear fender treatment, and a three-tiered vertical taillight treatment capped off the rear quarter. Virgil Exner's design department had worked their magic and created a car that was pleasing to the eye with a graceful tailfin and a sweeping trim spear running the full length of the car. DeSoto was also catering to a broader market by offering several body styles including convertibles, family sedans, and beautiful station wagons as well. For 1956, a grand total of 12

The FireDome Series S-23 was powered by a 330.4-cubic-inch V-8 rated at 230 horsepower. This 2-door Sportsman model sold for $2,783 and rode on a 126-inch wheelbase. *From the Dennis David Collection*

models were available with seven in the S-23 FireDome Series and four regular models plus a special convertible available in the upper line S-24 Fireflite Series. A new feature this year was push-button controls on the dash. The driver had nothing more to do than to push the desired button in order to put the car in motion. A low gear and neutral were also provided, and the unique arrangement meant that the shifting lever was completely eliminated. Other engineering refinements for 1956 were an independent gas-fired heater, new 12-volt electrics, and even an option called the Highway HiFi that played its own set of special records spinning at 16-2/3 rpm. Also continued for 1956 was the Desotomatic steering wheel clock that was introduced in 1954. The clock would actually wind itself as the steering wheel was turned. With features such as these, DeSoto was everything a car should be for

1956. DeSoto would go on to produce a total of 109,442 cars for the 1956 model year.

After several concept cars carried the Adventurer name on the show circuit from 1953 to 1955, DeSoto was now ready to apply the name to a regular production automobile. For 1956, a new hardtop model called the Adventurer was introduced in the S-24 Series, and it featured spectacular performance. Here was a DeSoto built to display the performance capabilities of a powerful V-8 engine in a luxuriously appointed automobile. Power for the Adventurer came from a 341-cubic-inch V-8 that was modified by enlarging the cylinder bore, then increasing the compression ratio to 9.25:1. A high-lift camshaft and a modified intake manifold topped off with twin four-barrel carburetors gave the Adventurer V-8 a whopping 320 horsepower. Available only in a 2-door hardtop and selling for $3,728, the

The station wagon in the FireDome Series had seating for six passengers with room to spare. *From the Dennis David Collection*

Adventurer was a true beauty queen. Only 996 were built for 1956.

DeSoto was also chosen as the Official Pace Car of the 1956 running of the Indianapolis 500, and two cars were custom-built for the race. Starting with a stock Fireflite convertible, DeSoto fitted the two cars with an engine, transmission, and suspension from the Adventurer, and then finished the padded dashboard with a gold colored fabric. All pace car replicas sold by DeSoto dealers were stock Fireflites fitted with a special trim package and suspension borrowed from the Adventurer. The glamorous Adventurer was also given the status of "Official car" for the event as well. The honor of driving the pace car was given to DeSoto Division president Irving Woolson, who had spent many years as an engineer with DeSoto. Pat Flaherty driving for John Zink Jr. won the race, and Flaherty averaged 128 miles per hour.

The top-of-the-line Adventurer would have surely been chosen as the 1956 Indianapolis Pace Car, but that honor went to the Fireflite convertible because the Adventurer was available only as a hardtop for 1956.

With the exception of the Australian-built cars, both the U.S. DeSoto and the export Diplomat lost their teeth for 1956. In its place came a mesh design for the grille that featured a "V" in the center. The new "toothless" look made the DeSoto a bit more streamlined and the Diplomat actually took a step ahead with a tailfin that was a bit sharper than that of its U.S. based cousin. In a global economic move that was truly years ahead of its time, the Danish market even offered an economy model Diplomat that used a Perkins four-cylinder diesel engine.

Virgil Exner took DeSoto styling to new highs for 1957, and an all-new DeSoto greeted buyers for the model year. The triple taillight theme continued, but the upper bodyline was one clean sweep that ran the entire length of the car. The graceful tailfin treatment at the rear was an integral part of the body, and the new look was a design that the motoring public loved. The Adventurer received four headlights for 1957, as this feature became legal in many states. DeSoto actually came very close to beating Chrysler's output this year, as 117,747 units were built against Chrysler's 118,733 cars for the calendar year. For 1957, DeSoto offered the S-25 FireDome, the S-26 Fireflite, the S-27 Firesweep, and the S-26A Adventurer. There were a multitude of body styles available for 1957, with the FireDome available in a 2- or 4-door Sportsman model, plus a sedan and convertible in the line-up. The Fireflite featured a grand total of six models that paralleled the FireDome, plus two station wagons with seating for six or nine passengers.

The Adventurer started the year as a hardtop only, but a convertible was introduced before the year was out. The hefty price tag of $4,272 meant that only 300 Adventurer convertibles were built. The Adventurer also set a milestone in 1957, as it was the first U.S. production car to produce one horsepower per cubic inch in stock form. The standard Adventurer came with the 345-cubic-inch dual-quad Hemi V-8 that generated 345 horsepower. Although Chevrolet advertised the same claim, their 283-cubic-inch V-8 required the optional fuel injection to make this claim. The Adventurer actually out-powered the Chevrolet V-8 by 62 horsepower. DeSoto's limited advertising budget dictated that this important innovation went largely unnoticed by the general public, and 1957 would also be the last year that DeSoto would use the Hemi engine.

Enhancing DeSoto's sales for 1957 was the introduction of a new low-priced DeSoto that enticed buyers to the showrooms. Selling for only $2,777 in sedan form, the Firesweep Series that was officially known as the S-27 was offered in five different models ranging from a 2-door hardtop to a nine-passenger station wagon. The Firesweep line was actually built by Dodge on Dodge's 122-inch wheelbase, and was powered by a 325-cubic-inch Wedge V-8, while all other DeSoto's used the Hemi engine. The affordable Firesweep line accounted for a major percentage of DeSoto's sales for 1957. Overall, DeSoto's offerings for 1957 had all of the bases covered, and with alluring names like Sportsman, Shopper, Explorer, and Adventurer, there was something in DeSoto's line for everyone. The introduction of the Firesweep line also added a somewhat strange hierarchy to the pricing structure for DeSoto, as there was now a definite low, medium, and high priced car within the line-up. Adding to this was the ultimate top-of-the-line Adventurer, which seemed to be competing with the likes of Cadillac. The line also featured an offering of "specialty cars" from DeSoto. Hearses, flower cars, ambulances, and even limousines were available, although they were all special order vehicles. DeSoto's limousine was only available through the Fleet Sales Department. It was basically a Fireflite 4-door sedan stretched by three feet with two more doors added. The conversion was made by the Memphis Coach Company, and many of these long wheelbase cars found favor with airports and tourist companies.

The Highway HiFi continued as a factory or dealer-installed option until early 1957, when the option was discontinued due to service problems. Dealers continued to install them until 1959 when their inventories were used up.

The Diplomat was also completely changed for 1957, as it now used a front end borrowed directly from DeSoto's Firesweep line. This marked the first time that the DeSoto and

A mere push of the button was all it took to place the 1956 Fireflite in motion. It was billed as "Magic Touch," and was a standard feature in the Fireflite Series, but was a $189 option in the FireDome line. *From the Les Pesavento Collection*

the Diplomat shared a common look in their front-end styling. The rear was still Plymouth-based all the way, and the unique blend of the two bodies made for an attractive car. The Diplomat also carried a Plymouth-based interior with the DeSoto name embossed on the dash.

DeSoto truly offered an astounding number of different models for 1957, and if a multitude of models and prices were not enough, pricing within Chrysler's family of cars added even more complications and confusion to the mix. There were overlaps in many divisions that left many buyers scratching their heads over which one to buy. DeSoto rested somewhere in-between Chrysler and Dodge, with Plymouth holding down the low-priced market.

The Firesweep was DeSoto's attempt to create a low-, medium-, and high-priced car within its own series. The most expensive model,

the nine-passenger wagon, sold for $3,310, a figure that was well into the territory of the mid-priced FireDome line. The introduction of the lower priced Firesweep line helped DeSoto place 11th in the industry for 1957, which would go on record as DeSoto's third best year in its history. It was an irony that would be bittersweet in the end. The crowded U.S. automobile market was still taking its victims. Before the decade was over, great names like Nash, Hudson, and Kaiser would be gone. Even the once great Packard would take its last breaths of life as a mere shadow of its former self. Clearly the post-World War II market had become saturated, and the weaker car companies were falling victim to market factors. With DeSoto's great cars and super sales for 1957, no one could have foreseen what was just around the corner. In a few short years, the death knell would also ring for the great DeSoto.

FireSweep 4-door *Sportsman*

Virgil Exner took styling to its absolute pinnacle for 1957 with a whole new look. While the Fireflite was still the top-of-the-line model, DeSoto also introduced the low-priced Firesweep line based on the Dodge chassis. *From the Les Pesavento Collection*

The new Firesweep line included two wagons called the "Explorer" and the "Shopper." The Explorer featured a third seat in the rear for more passengers, while the Shopper used the space for cargo. *From the Les Pesavento Collection*

TWO NEW FIRESWEEP 4-DOOR STATION WAGONS

FIRESWEEP *Shopper* (illustrated above)   FIRESWEEP *Explorer*

A DeSoto factory photo collage for 1957 shows the unique styling features offered. DeSoto had a banner year in 1957 with 117,747 cars built for the calendar year. *From the Les Pesavento Collection*

DE SOTO

quality and distinction

CHRYSLER

ANOTHER CHRYSLER FIRST

FIRST IN THE COUPE UTILITY FIELD TO OFFER THE CHOICE OF FULL TIME POWER STEERING, AUTOMATIC OVERDRIVE, FULLY AUTOMATIC TRANSMISSION.

in Australia's newest, finest, passenger-car

COUPE UTILITY

DeSotos built in Australia had taken their own paths and were still using the U.S. dies from the 1954 line. For 1956-1957, the Australian UTE was a popular car Down Under. *Society of Automotive Historians, Dunwoodie Archives/AACA Library and Research Center*

DeSoto continued its successful taxi cab business for 1957 with an offering based on its Firesweep line. The taxi was a unique offering in that it used a six-cylinder engine while other domestic DeSotos used an eight. *From the Doug Dressler Collection*

DeSoto DIVISION OF CHRYSLER CORPORATION

DE SOTO MOTOR CARS • FIREFLITE V8 • FIREDOME V8

P. O. BOX 1628 • DETROIT 31, MICHIGAN

June 10, 1957

TO ALL DE SOTO DEALERS:

Recently a bulletin was sent to you describing prices and specifications for the De Soto 6-cylinder Taxicab. This vehicle is now available and may be ordered through your normal channels.

The attached picture will give you a good idea why cab owners will
like the style of this vehicle. It offers them a heavier, more
luxurious vehicle at a competitive price for such uses as airport
and terminal service. Our experience with these 1957 De Soto cabs
points up two very interesting things. First: The majority of our
cabs are being purchased by individual driver-owners. They're your
best prospects. Second: Many of our cabs are being ordered with
power brakes and automatic transmissions. Don't overlook these
profitable extras.

If you need any help on specifications or bids the Regional Office is
prepared to offer assistance.

Sincerely,

J. B. Wagstaff
Vice President
DE SOTO DIVISION

Att.
DS-744

14733

DESIGNED FOR THE SUPERHIGHWAY AGE

A letter dated June 10, 1957 from DeSoto Vice-President J.B. Wagstaff announced the availability of the DeSoto taxi for 1957. The letter states that individual cab owners are DeSoto's biggest market. *From the Doug Dressler Collection*

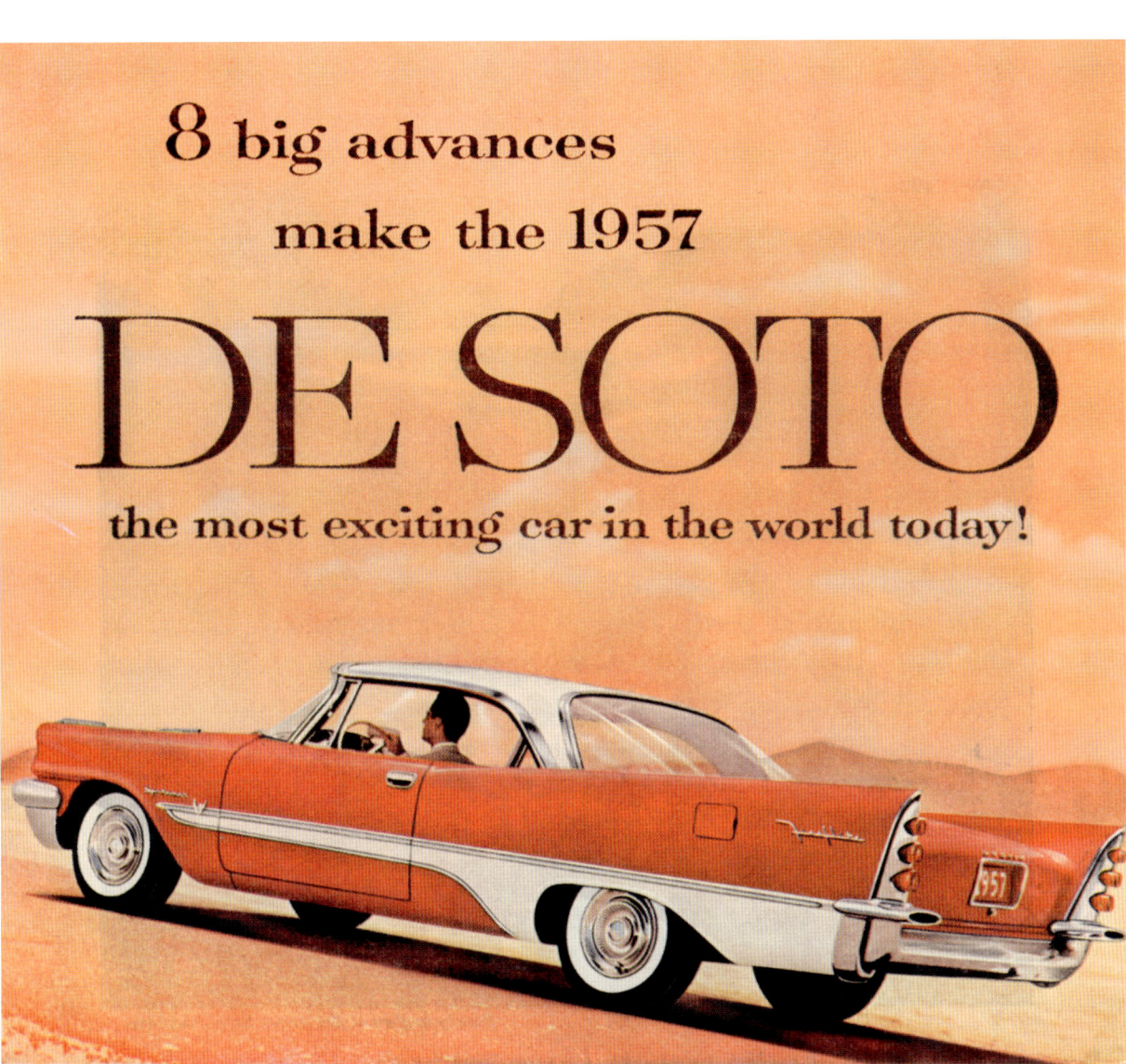

8 big advances make the 1957

DE SOTO

the most exciting car in the world today!

DE SOTO DIVISION, CHRYSLER CORPORATION

New *Torsion-Aire* ride! De Soto for '57 has a completely new suspension combining torsion bars, outrider springs and super-soft cushion tires. It gives you an exciting level ride, corners without lean or sway, and prevents "dive" on quick stops.

New *TorqueFlite* transmission! Most advanced transmission built, TorqueFlite gives a smooth flow of power and exciting new getaway.

New *Triple-Range* push-button control! Simply touch a button of De Soto's new Triple-Range push button, and—presto—you're on your way! Positive mechanical control.

New *Flight Sweep* styling—the new shape of motion—upswept tail fins; lower-than-ever lines; plenty of head-room and 32% more windshield area!

New super-powered V-8 engines! '57 De Soto engines are powerful, efficient, and rugged—respond instantly for quick, safe passing. Your choice of 3 mighty V-8's!

New *4-Season* air conditioner! This compact unit—mounted out of the way under the dash—*cools* in summer, *heats* in winter. Removes dust and pollen. One simple set of controls.

New glamorous interiors! Each '57 De Soto interior features luxurious and durable new fabrics with smart accenting trim and a beautiful new flight-styled instrument panel.

New advanced power features! You can have your choice of the finest power features ever offered in an automobile! See the new De Soto at your De Soto-Plymouth dealer's.

WIDE NEW PRICE RANGE...STARTS CLOSE TO THE LOWEST!

FireSweep—big-value new-comer for 1957—priced just above the lowest. 245 hp

Firedome—medium-priced pacemaker in 1957—exciting style and performance. 270 hp

Fireflite—high-powered luxury for 1957—the last word in design and power. 295 hp

De Soto dealers present **Groucho Marx** in "You Bet Your Life" on NBC radio and TV

An ad proudly announces eight big innovations for 1957, one of which was a new four season air-conditioning system. *From the Les Pesavento Collection*

Chapter 6

FROM GLORY TO DEATH

The U.S. economy took a nosedive in 1958, and the automobile industry was hit especially hard. Times were changing, and the extravagant excesses of the 1950s were beginning to wane. There was a change in the air: a change that would soon call for more streamlining and fuel efficiency in the design of the U.S. automobile. This change was no more evident than in the fact that Rambler's new downsized model called the "American" was the only U.S. auto model to make gains in the market for 1958. In a few years, this new type of smaller car would show up in many forms as the Plymouth Valiant, Oldsmobile F-85, Buick Special,

Pontiac Tempest, Chevrolet Corvair, and the Ford Falcon. While these cars could have sold well in 1958, they were only on the drawing boards at a time when the recession-wracked economy wanted nothing to do with the huge automobiles that Detroit was producing.

DeSoto made only slight variations to its offerings for 1958, and the focus was not really on the cars themselves, but what was happening behind the scenes. The Chrysler Corporation was rearranging its production strategy, and this would be the last year that DeSotos would be built at their own plant. By the middle of the year, DeSoto production had ceased at its Wyoming Avenue and McGraw Road plants, and other Chrysler manufacturing endeavors had moved in. The recession of 1958, coupled with quality control problems, made

FIREDOME CONVERTIBLE

The LS2-M FireDome convertible was a streamlined car from front to back. It sold for $3,489 and only 519 were built. *From the Dennis David Collection*

"I am convinced that the De Soto Dealer Announcement Meeting last month was the kick-off of a fine business year.

Everywhere there is growing enthusiasm, confidence and optimism. Our 1959 Dealer Meeting was a spectacular expression of the wonderful enthusiasm and optimism and vitality of you De Soto dealers.

This turnout has great significance for us at De Soto and throughout the Corporation. It also has significance to Detroit and the automobile industry.

This meeting is viewed as a dramatic and spectacular vote of confidence not just for De Soto, but for the entire industry.

And there are other strong reasons for confidence. More people are working right now than in 1955 when we sold 7.2 million. Incomes—after taxes—are at an all-time high, averaging $5,300.

Savings banks are loaded, with 304 billion dollars available.

We have a fine year coming up, and we face it with a magnificent new De Soto. You are a great selling organization, and you've proved this, year after year, for 30 years.

We are on the glory road — and nothing can stop us.

Good selling."

J. B. Wagstaff

J. B. WAGSTAFF
General Manager,
DE SOTO DIVISION

DE SOTO 1929 1959

1929 1959 *Retailer*

OCTOBER, 1958   **DE SOTO DIVISION**

DeSoto staged a two-day promotional event for their dealers as a way to introduce the 1959 models. The gathering attracted nearly 4,000 people and at the end over 1,500 DeSotos were driven back to the dealerships. *From the Lee Exline collection*

For 1958, DeSoto dealers were able to offer a number of conversions for professional use in the line-up. The Briarean line from the Richard Brothers in Eaton Rapids, Michigan, featured a raised roof. *From the Doug Dressler Collection*

for a year that was not kind to DeSoto, and production numbers proved it. DeSoto's high-end Adventurer sold a mere 82 convertibles for 1958, and even its affordable 4-door sedan in the Firesweep line sold just 7,646 units. Accordingly, Dodge and Chrysler production also lost ground in 1958, but not to the extent of DeSoto. It seemed that DeSoto was being pushed out of the market from the outside as well as from within. Posting its worst year since 1938, DeSoto production had begun its downward spiral, and like a mortally wounded warplane, there would be no recovery.

Despite the warmed-over styling for 1958, DeSoto still marketed a multitude of cars that offered motorists everything they needed in a car. Series designations once again changed with the lower line Firesweep now known as

the Series LS1-L, the FireDome known as the LS2-M, and the Fireflite became the LS3-H. The prestigious and upscale high-end Adventurer became the LS3-S, and again was available as a hardtop or convertible. A bright spot in the 1958 line-up was DeSoto's new V-8 engines. Advantages such as lighter weight, improved engine accessibility, cylindrical wedge combustion chambers, and a new carburetor that featured the "Econo-Choke" promised better performance while saving gas. The low-priced Firesweep line used a 350-cubic-inch V-8, while all others received the larger bore 361. Still in a class by itself was the Adventurer, which featured a pair of four-barrel carburetors, high performance camshaft and valve gearing, and dual exhausts. A Bendix electronic fuel-injection system was offered as an option, but very few were built, and all were recalled and retrofitted with dual four-barrel carburetors because of service problems related to the electronics.

DeSoto also contracted with several companies for conversion of its station wagons for ambulance and professional work for 1958. In January of that year, DeSoto announced the offering of its Fireflite and Firesweep Station Wagons as Utility cars for all professional needs. The wagons were available from the Richard Brothers Allied Products Corporation in Eaton Rapids, Michigan, and from the National Body Corporation in Detroit, Michigan. The conversions featured a raised roof that offered easier access and more maneuverability inside the car. The Richard Brothers conversion was called the "Briarean Line," and a DeSoto company memo from J. B. Wagstaff featured capital letters stating that the use of the TorqueFlite transmission, power brakes, and a 40-amp generator was strongly recommended. A multitude of options were also available for the wagons including a two-man resuscitator with demand inhaler

DESOTO MOTOR CARS

DESOTO DIVISION OF CHRYSLER CORPORATION

P. O. BOX 1628 • DETROIT 31, MICHIGAN

January 23, 1958

TO ALL DE SOTO DEALERS:

Attached is literature concerning a new conversion now available for the De Soto Fireflite Station Wagon. "The Briarean Line" may be fitted as an ambulance or hearse and features a roof which has been raised approximately 6 inches. This modification provides more headroom which permits easier access to the rear compartment and more freedom of movement. Added head-room is particularly useful in the handling of heart patients and others who must be moved in a semi-vertical position.

You should find this conversion of considerable interest to Funeral Directors, Hospitals, Ambulance Service Companies, Civil Defense Organizations, Municipal Aid Stations and Governmental, Utility and Industrial Plants with medical or First Aid facilities. It will be well worth your time to solicit their business.

All modifications required can be made on the De Soto Fireflite Station Wagons. Either 2-seat or 3-seat models may be used. Since De Soto does not make the actual modifications, all orders for the conversion should be placed directly with Mr. W. J. James, Plant Manager, Allied Products Corporation, Box 48, Eaton Rapids, Michigan.

All orders for the De Soto Shopper or Explorer Station Wagons should be pro-cessed through your regular channels with specific instructions to complete the Briarean 6" roof modification at the factory and to deliver the vehicles to Allied Products Corporation for completion. The destination charge to Eaton Rapids is #39.50. Ultimate transportation to the dealer will be coordinated by Allied Products Corporation and charged by them to the dealer.

IT IS STRONGLY RECOMMENDED THAT POWER BRAKES BE ORDERED WITH THIS PACKAGE. IF ANY HEAVY DUTY ELECTRICAL EQUIPMENT SUCH AS SIRENS, WARNING LIGHTS OR ADDITIONAL INTERIOR LIGHTS ARE ADDED, A 40-AMPERE HOUR GENERATOR IS RECOMMENDED.

Sincerely,

J. B. Wagstaff

J. B. Wagstaff
Vice President
DE SOTO DIVISION

Att.

21860

3 GREAT CARS • FIREFLITE • FIREDOME • FIRESWEEP

A letter dated January 23, 1958, from DeSoto Vice President J. B. Wagstaff strongly advised that all profes-sional cars be fitted with power brakes and a 40-ampere generator. *From the Doug Dressler Collection*

FIREFLITE 4 DOOR SHOPPER

FIRESWEEP 4 DOOR EXPLORER

FIRESWEEP 4 DOOR SHOPPER

DeSoto offered wagons in all of its series for 1958. The most expensive was the Fireflite nine-passenger wagon selling for $4,172. *From the Dennis David Collection*

priced at $440, a rather hefty option for any car. Another conversion was available from the Memphis Coachworks as an ambulance built on the Firesweep sedan. The conversion featured a completely customized rear section and roof that drastically altered the rear section of the entire car. Several of the Memphians have survived, but they are rare sights at car shows in the present day.

DeSoto used a rather unique marketing tool for 1958 that resulted in one of the rarest of all DeSotos ever built. Known formally as the Firemite, it was a 3/8-scaled replica of the 1958 DeSoto Fireflite convertible. Power for the Firemite came from a two-horsepower Briggs & Stratton engine, and it even had a six-volt battery for the lights. Firemites were shipped to

Used as a dealer promotional tool in 1958, the DeSoto Firemite was built by the Robel Corporation of Berwick, PA and powered by a two-horsepower Briggs & Stratton engine. The little Firemites were highly successful in having children drag their parents to DeSoto showrooms. *Original artwork by John Satterthwaite*

The Adventurer featured swivel seats for easy entrance and egress. *From the Les Pesavento Collection*

dealers where they attracted a lot of attention. Some dealers even loaded the Firemite into the back of a truck where it was transported to the local elementary school during recess. Tickets were then handed out for a free "test drive" of the Firemite, which resulted in children relentlessly hounding their parents to take them to the dealership. Unsuspecting parents waiting for their children's turn at the Firemite then made for easy targets of a sales pitch for the 1958 DeSoto line-up. The Firemites were very successful in creating foot traffic to dealer showrooms, and are very rare today.

The Diplomat line again used a Firesweep front end with a Plymouth body, and now featured dual headlamps just like the U.S. based Firesweep model. There were a few enhancements made to the Diplomat's offerings, as buyers could choose from several different engines ranging from the trusty six-cylinder to a plethora of V-8s. The entire Diplomat line consisted of sedans, hardtops, wagons, and convertibles. Unfortunately for the Diplomat, it suffered the same fate as its U.S. counterpart for 1958, and only 3,250 were built. In Australia, the Diplomat that was based on the 1954 styling was terminated, and the Firesweep Series was available in that country with right-hand drive.

Despite the rumors around Detroit of DeSoto's demise, the Chrysler Corporation put on a brave face and held a gala gathering of dealers in honor of DeSoto's 30th model year anniversary. Held in Detroit on September 22nd and 23rd of 1958, the event was billed as the largest dealer announcement ever staged by the automobile industry. The event was truly spectacular as nearly 4,000 dealers

The 1959 Adventurer convertible was an expensive car that sold for a whopping $4,749. Only 97 were built. *Photo by Dennis David*

and family members converged on the Motor City for the introduction of the 1959 models. The festivities featured a barbeque, banquets, and even a two-hour play appropriately called "Going Places," starring some of Broadway's finest performers. At the end of the two-day event, DeSoto dealers drove away over 1,500 new cars back to their dealerships. The event served to generate huge waves of enthusiasm for DeSoto's offerings for 1959.

With the exception of the Firesweep line being built at the Dodge plant, all DeSotos were built alongside Chryslers for 1959. While it was still a gorgeous car that commanded attention wherever it went, plans were being laid behind the scenes that would soon ring the death knell for DeSoto. Production numbers were not bringing in the dollars needed to justify its existence. Rumors were running rampant about the demise of DeSoto in Detroit's automotive circles. With many years of retrospect behind us, we can speculate on why DeSoto may have been targeted for termination. Of the four divisions, Chrysler certainly would not kill itself off as the namesake and flagship of the fleet; neither would the corporation terminate the bread and butter Plymouth line, which would receive the tremendously successful Valiant for 1961. (Chrysler introduced the Valiant in 1960, but did not designate it as part of the Plymouth line until 1961.) The lucky cousin Dodge, of which most of Chrysler's top management had been brought up through in their formative years, it was left as a sacred cow. This left no one watching out for the lone DeSoto, which was loosing ground every day. According to noted DeSoto authority Lee Exline, "This was a time of intense pressure from both inside and out for DeSoto, and no one had a vested interest in keeping DeSoto alive."

In spite of all of the darkness and gloom rumored around DeSoto in 1959, Virgil Exner still had big plans for the marque. According

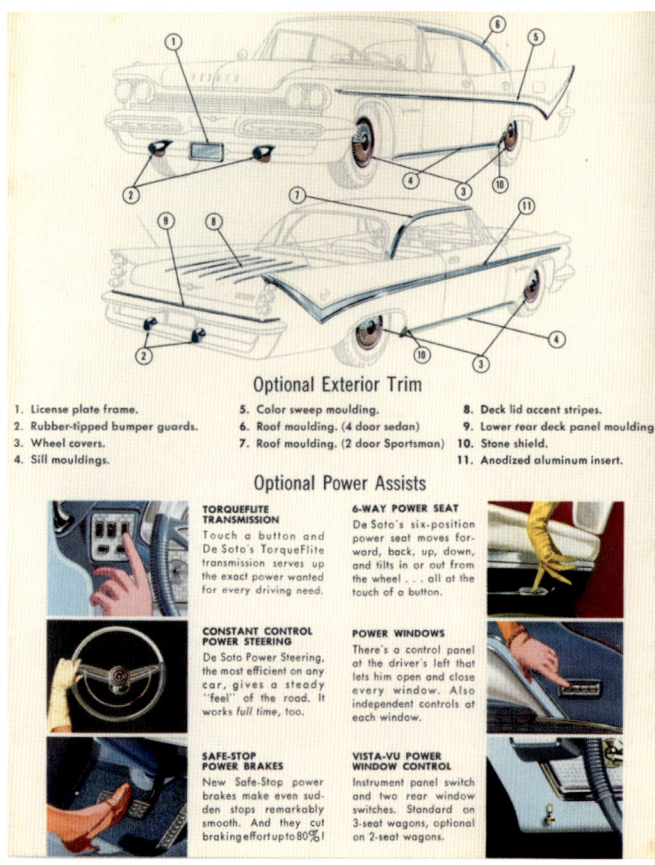

Optional Exterior Trim

1. License plate frame.
2. Rubber-tipped bumper guards.
3. Wheel covers.
4. Sill mouldings.
5. Color sweep moulding.
6. Roof moulding. (4 door sedan)
7. Roof moulding. (2 door Sportsman)
8. Deck lid accent stripes.
9. Lower rear deck panel moulding.
10. Stone shield.
11. Anodized aluminum insert.

Optional Power Assists

TORQUEFLITE TRANSMISSION
Touch a button and De Soto's TorqueFlite transmission serves up the exact power wanted for every driving need.

6-WAY POWER SEAT
De Soto's six-position power seat moves forward, back, up, down, and tilts in or out from the wheel . . . all at the touch of a button.

CONSTANT CONTROL POWER STEERING
De Soto Power Steering, the most efficient on any car, gives a steady "feel" of the road. It works *full time*, too.

POWER WINDOWS
There's a control panel at the driver's left that lets him open and close every window. Also independent controls at each window.

SAFE-STOP POWER BRAKES
New Safe-Stop power brakes make even sudden stops remarkably smooth. And they cut braking effort up to 80%!

VISTA-VU POWER WINDOW CONTROL
Instrument panel switch and two rear window switches. Standard on 3-seat wagons, optional on 2-seat wagons.

DeSoto offered a multitude of power assist and trim options for 1959, a year that featured a DeSoto for every purpose from basic transportation to luxury. *From the Dennis David Collection*

to noted historian Jeff Godshall, "Save for the Valiant/Lancer, all Chrysler Corporation cars were to be all-new for 1962, including DeSoto. These cars featured curved side glass and 'fuselage' styling and were intended to move the company beyond fins. This program was eventually killed, but not before a few prototypes were built, one of them a DeSoto, which was later cut up and scrapped."

Exner's version of DeSoto for 1962 was a model known as the "S" and development was well under way in May of 1959. A full-size clay mock-up of the "S" was radically different from anything previously seen—it featured a long hood/short rear deck theme. Exner actually developed the design in his

"special room," and very few were allowed to see it. In the end, the design never reached the production stage, but Exner did manage to come up with a new DeSoto dream car for 1959. Introduced at the Chicago Auto Show, and known as the Cella I, it featured a futuristic body and proposed the use of alternative power in the form of a fuel cell that combined hydrogen and oxygen gases to create electricity. The electricity was then used to drive one motor on each wheel. Advantages of the Cella I's power source were said to be maximum acceleration and traction potential, smooth and quiet operation, and no transmission, driveshaft, or rear axle. Sadly, the Cella I never made it past a 3/8-scale model, and a working prototype was never built. In the present day, several car companies in the global market are developing hydrogen-powered cars, something that DeSoto proposed many decades earlier with the innovative Cella I.

DeSoto again offered a multitude of body styles in four series of cars for 1959: the Series MS1-L Firesweep, the MS2-M Series Fire-Dome, the MS3-H Fireflite, plus the top-of-the-line Adventurer. The entry level Firesweep featured six body styles including a convertible and station wagon, and before the year was out two new Seville hardtops were added to the line. The FireDome Series offered four choices, and the two Seville hardtops were added to this line as well. The Fireflite Series still offered a convertible and station wagon for a total of six body styles. The Adventurer maintained its offerings of the 2-door coupe and convertible only. A swivel seat that made for easy exit and entry was available as a standard feature on the Adventurer, and it was an option in the rest of the line. Other amenities for 1959 were an optional Automatic headlight beam changer that sensed an oncoming car and switched to low beam by itself, and a "Mirror-Matic" rearview mirror that automatically adjusted itself

DE SOTO CELLA I Though not a true full-sized Idea Car, the Cella I predicted in 3/8 scale the appearance of a future car that would be powered by a new type of power plant, the fuel cell. In this power system, the interaction of hydrogen and oxygen gases in a cell converts directly to electrical energy, which is used to drive lightweight, high-speed electric motors geared to each of the four wheels. Among the advantages: maximum acceleration and traction potential; quiet, extra-smooth operation; eliminates transmission, drive shaft, and rear axle. De Soto engineers introduced the Cella I at the 1959 Chicago Auto Show.

In a look to the future that is still being explored today, DeSoto introduced the Cella I in 1959. The experimental vehicle used a cell that combined hydrogen and oxygen to produce electricity. Sadly, the Cella I never made it past a 3/8-scale mock up, and a working prototype was never built. *From the Les Pesavento Collection*

Adventurer 4-door hardtop

You demand a distinctive automobile that still is easy to get in and out of
and has room for the entire family. *You* demand the Adventurer
4-door hardtop! It has inches more room inside (as much room as the
4-door sedan!) and all the glamour of the magic name "Adventurer."

An Adventurer 4-door hardtop is pictured next to a rocket in this artist's rendering from 1960. The tripletail light theme from 1959 had now been replaced by a single tail lamp lens. *From the Les Pesavento Collection*

to prevent rearview glare. Air suspension was also offered on the rear only, and 1959 would be the only year for this option.

The 1959 models represented a number of "lasts" for DeSoto. This would be the last year for a convertible and station wagon (except for the foreign Diplomat), and 1959 would also be the last year for the body-on-frame construction, as all DeSotos for 1960 would feature a new unit-body. DeSoto built its two-millionth car in 1959, and one could only speculate at this point if more advertising from Chrysler could have saved it. Sadly, 1959 would be a dismal year for the once proud company with total production standing at only 40,058 cars for the calendar year. Only the Imperial figured less in the Chrysler family with a mere 17,268 cars built. Given the Imperial's lofty price tag, its low production numbers were perhaps justified in the Chrysler line-up, but with a multitude of models available from DeSoto, the production model breakdown for sales was not impressive.

As a new decade dawned the smaller car phenomenon had taken hold of the U.S. automobile market. The big news from Chrysler was the Valiant, which sold 146,792 units for 1960. Ford's Falcon, which was introduced a year before, sold an incredible 466,240 cars. The introduction of the Falcon in 1959 had shattered the record that DeSoto had held since its introduction back in 1928. Clearly, America was looking for a new type of car, and DeSoto had nothing to offer.

For 1960, the writing was on the wall and parent Chrysler had paired DeSoto's offerings down to only two series. The Firesweep and FireDome were dropped, and the formerly upper-line Fireflite became the Series PS1-L low-priced offering from DeSoto. The once pedigreed Adventurer became the PS3-M and was no longer a luxury offering, as it was paired down to medium price status. There

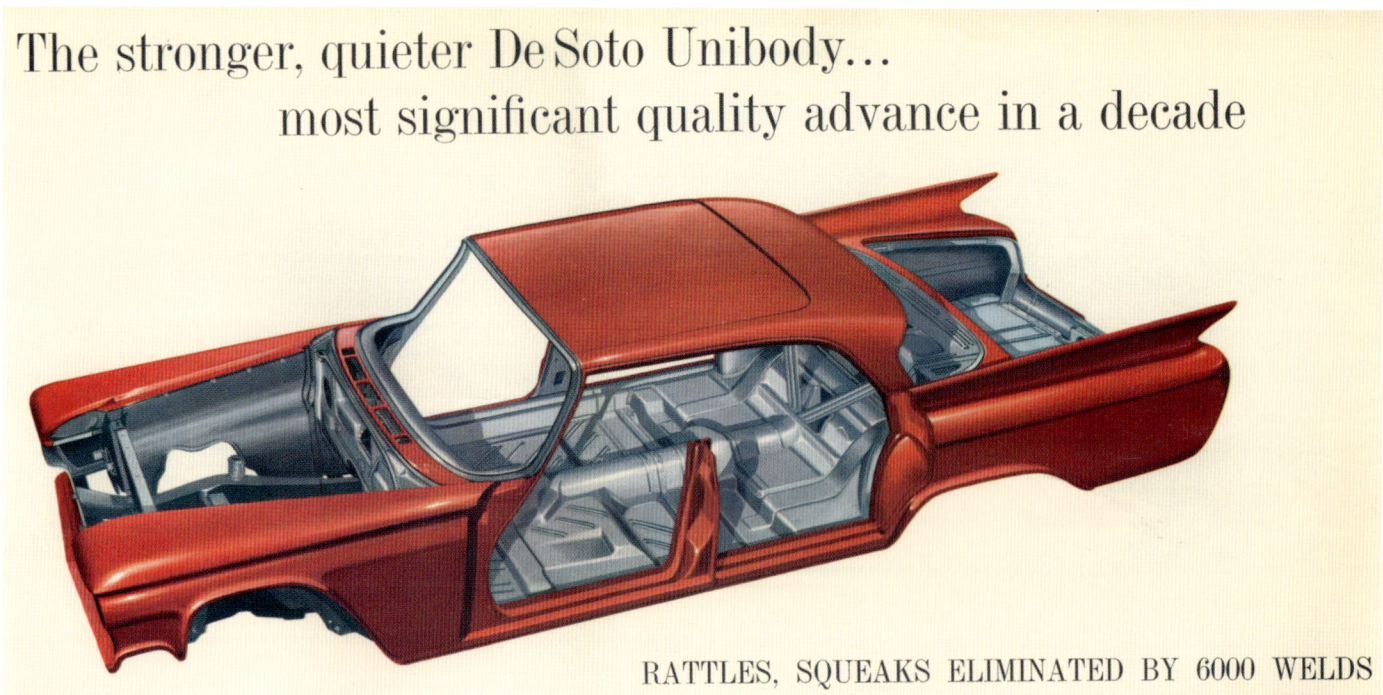

The stronger, quieter De Soto Unibody...
most significant quality advance in a decade

RATTLES, SQUEAKS ELIMINATED BY 6000 WELDS

All DeSotos for 1960 featured new unitized bodies that eliminated the need for a frame. Unitized bodies offered increased strength and rattle-free motoring, even on the toughest roads. *From the Les Pesavento Collection*

Fireflite 4-door sedan

DeSoto was clearly trying to tie its new cars in with state-of-the-art technology, as this factory brochure from 1960 features a supersonic jet in the background. A Fireflite 4-door sedan is pictured. *From the Les Pesavento Collection*

were three models available in each series, and although styling was all-new, it did little to impress the motoring public. Power for the Fireflite Series came from DeSoto's 1959 Firesweep Turbo-flash V-8 rated at 295 horsepower. The Adventurer's engine was reduced to the previous year's FireDome unit, but was available in two options known as the Mark I and the Ram Charge. The more potent of the two was the Ram Charge, which offered dual four-barrel carburetors and ram induction manifolds boosting the Adventurer's output to an impressive 330 horsepower. The huge tailfin that had literally defined the latter 1950s was on its way out, and DeSoto now shared its bodies with the 122-inch-wheelbase Chrysler line. Only 26,081 DeSotos left the factory in 1960, and rumors were running rampant in Detroit's inner circles of the marque's demise. With most automakers posting production numbers in the 100,000s, it was clear that DeSoto was not cutting it in the market.

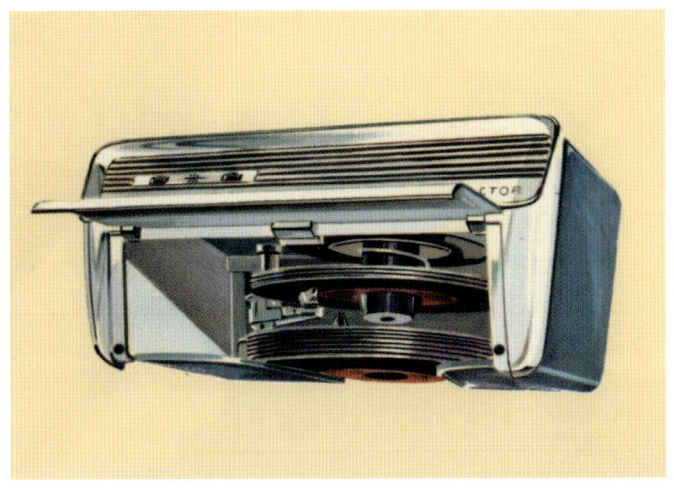

Built for DeSoto by RCA, the Ultra-Fi record player could play two hours of music by stacking up 45-rpm records. It was an extra cost option. *From the Les Pesavento Collection*

All vestiges of the homogenized Diplomat were now gone, as the Diplomat for 1960 was now merely a Dodge Dart wearing DeSoto badges with side trim reminiscent of the 1957 DeSoto. Because the Diplomat was now based on a standard production Dodge, it was available in convertible, hardtop, sedan, and wagon form. Power for the Diplomat was also available in six- or eight-cylinder engines. Such a variety of offerings were something its U.S. based cousin could only dream of, and DeSoto entered its last year as a mere shadow of its former self.

There was only one series offered in 1961, DeSoto's last year. Officially known as the

DeSoto's offering had been reduced to just one model for 1961, the company's last year. It was simply called "DeSoto." *From the Les Pesavento Collection*

Even though it was in its last year, the DeSoto 4-door hardtop still struck an impressive pose. *Photo by Dennis David*

1961 would be the last year of Virgil Exner's styling influence for DeSoto and the Chrysler camp. The 1960s would usher in a new era, but DeSoto would not be a part of it. This rear quarter shot shows the true beauty inherent in DeSoto's final year. *Photo by Dennis David*

RS1-L, it didn't even warrant a model name. It was simply called a DeSoto. Available in only 2- and 4-door hardtops, it was basically a warmed over 1960 model with a little rework on the front-end. Virgil Exner's styling influence was over, and his tenure as Director of Styling at Chrysler would end shortly after DeSoto production came to a halt. There was also a big shake up in management at Chrysler during 1961, and before the year was over a number of executives were gone. Even the office of President of the Chrysler Corporation sat vacant for several months after a scandal involving William C. Newberg left no one at the helm. The only winner in DeSoto's last year was the new Valiant, which was absorbed into the Plymouth line for 1961. Many historians have speculated on DeSoto's future had

DE SOTO

FOR NINETEEN SIXTY-ONE...
and then there were NONE!

The general acceptance of DeSoto's 1961 model was not held in high regard by the motoring public as the end was clearly in sight. Although a stylish car, only 911 two-doors were built before the line closed down for good. *Artwork by John Satterthwaite*

the name been assigned to the Valiant, but with Chrysler's management troubles taking center stage at the time, a new and smaller DeSoto was never considered. Although not unexpected by most, DeSoto's demise must have come as a surprise to some. History shows that there were drawings on the table for a 1964 U.S. DeSoto, and there were also full-size clay proposals and metal prototypes in the design studios for 1962 and 1963 models. These renderings of a future DeSoto would never see the light of day, and in the end only 3,034 units were built before the line was shut down. The car that had once captured the very essence of the American motoring spirit was gone.

Certainly DeSoto can be credited with pioneering several design concepts for the Chrysler camp. The famous Miller racecar-inspired grilles of 1932 and 1933 were great looking cars, and the unique Airflow design that was DeSoto's own for 1934 was a virtual test bed of unique ideas. The hidden headlamps on the 1942 S-10 models were years ahead of their time, and DeSoto showed the American family how to travel in style with the giant Suburbans of the postwar era. Towards the end, the stunning Adventurer pioneered the concept of luxury and performance, all in the same package.

The fact that there even was a DeSoto offered for the 1961 model year amazed many in Detroit, as rumors of its ultimate demise had been openly discussed for several years. According to retired Chrysler engineer Eugene Weiss, "There would not have been a DeSoto for 1961 had it not been for the fact

DeSoto's Ghost Haunts Chrysler

The ghost of DeSoto is haunting Chrysler Corp. in the form of a decision the Supreme Court has refused to review. Since the decision of a lower court is now left standing, it means Chrysler is responsible for damages to dealers as a result of dropping the production of DeSotos six years ago.

Some of the 35 dealer suits are asking more than $1 million in damages and that's enough to cause great gnashing of teeth by the 1,500 dealers who have not instituted litigation. The statute of limitations apparently bars future suits, and there will be many disgruntled DeSoto, Kaiser-Frazer and Packard dealers who would like to turn back the clock.

It is possible, however, that other dealer contracts were more far-sighted than the DeSoto arrangement. The court found the contract permitted Chrysler to drop model lines and body types, but not entire makes or brands of cars. Dealers can be sure today that the automotive companies will be carefully checking the fine print in each dealer contract.

If the Edsel dealer contracts had omitted the "make or brand" clause, the effect probably would have been nullified by Ford's timely offer to allow these unfortunate dealers the option of selling other Ford brands. Undoubtedly when the Edsel was laid to rest management wanted it to stay buried.

The contract loophole in the DeSoto decision does raise one more irreverent question. Is it possible the DeSoto contract lawyers are the same ones who put General Motor's hired gumshoes on Ralph Nader?

Ancient sculpture, coins and manuscripts show juggling to be an old art. We thought the skill originated with the issuance of checkbooks.

HARVEY PATTON

Many DeSoto dealers filed lawsuits over the demise of the marque, and a Supreme Court decision in 1966 upheld their right to damages. This article is from the December 8, 1966, issue of the *Detroit News*. *National Automotive History Collection, Detroit Public Library*

that parts had to be ordered three months ahead of time." Chrysler was also faced with a budget problem of how to fund production of its hugely successful Valiant. In the end, the DeSoto was built until all of the parts were used up and the last DeSoto, a turquoise and white 2-door hardtop, was driven off the line on November 30, 1960. With it went the 32-year production run of one of America's most memorable cars.

The great explorer Hernando de Soto died of a fever on May 21, 1542, on the banks of the Mississippi River. The DeSoto Division of Chrysler died on a piece of paper dated November 18, 1960. It was certainly not a fitting end for either. After bearing such wonderful names as Adventurer, Sportsman, Fireflite, FireDome, Firesweep, Coronado, and the wonderful CF and S-Series cars, the DeSoto name was gone. It is ironic that Chrysler introduced the new Newport model in the same year as the DeSoto Division's demise. The Newport would sell a respectable 83,120 units in 1962, and even Dodge got its own replacement for the DeSoto in the form of the 880 model for 1962. Was DeSoto strangled from within, and did Chrysler plan to replace the DeSoto with the Chrysler Newport all along? These are questions that many have speculated on, and opinions will be offered until the end of time. According to automotive historian Kit Foster, "The Chrysler Newport, although not as well appointed as the DeSoto, basically took DeSoto's place, and showed there was still a market for such a car. The Newport sold well enough in 1961, over 57,000 cars, that Dodge dealers demanded one too." Clearly there was a market for a car like DeSoto in the early 1960s, as evidenced by the success of Chrysler's Newport and the Dodge 880.

For the most part, production of the Diplomat also ended in 1961, although a Diplomat was still available for 1962 in South Africa. Available only as a 4-door sedan, it was shipped in a knockdown format and assembled there. Sales of a car called the DeSoto Rebel also continued for 1963 and 1964, as 4-door Dodge Lancers were assembled in Africa and affixed with DeSoto Rebel nameplates.

The DeSoto name was still available in various places around the globe for a few more years as re-badged Dodge trucks, and the DeSoto name lives on to this very day in the form of trucks built in Turkey; although the venture has severed its ties with the DaimlerChrysler Corporation. Certainly the passing of DeSoto closed a chapter of American automotive history that will never be seen again. Quite simply, it was Delightful, it was Delovely, it was DeSoto.

EPILOGUE

They gather once every year, and they call themselves the National DeSoto Club. They come from places like Akron, Ohio, Seattle, Washington, Mountain Lakes, New Jersey, Mount Pleasant, South Carolina, Ontario, Canada, and even Prescott, Merseyside, England. They gather not to commemorate the death of the wonderful DeSoto, but to celebrate its life and its very existence. Born in the infancy of the Great Depression, DeSoto went on to become a car for all of America, but in the end it could not define itself in the marketplace. Taken over by its bigger brother Chrysler, it didn't go down without a fight. Indeed, many DeSoto dealers filed lawsuits when their franchises were closed, and it took many years of courtroom battles to settle the lawsuits; but settled they were and even though some rulings were favorable to the franchises, the American DeSoto never came back. In name only they were produced in several places around the world after 1961. For 1963, there was even a DeSoto Rebel available in South Africa, and the Chrysler Corporation even applied the DeSoto name to a line of foreign trucks, but again they were in name only. There was nothing specific about it that made it a unique vehicle that could truly wear Hernando's name, or capture the spirit of exploration and adventure that the true DeSoto had.

Photo by Dennis David/2005 National DeSoto Convention-St. Catherine's, Ontario, Canada

Photo by Dennis David/2005 National DeSoto Convention-St. Catherine's, Ontario, Canada

But all of the controversy over the death of DeSoto is not why the National DeSoto Club gathers. Their yearly convention ensures that all will remember a car that America came to know and love, and it also helps to introduce a whole new generation of newcomers to the marque. Some years ago, many members would be heard to say, "My father had a DeSoto." Today one is more likely to hear worlds like, "My grandfather owned a DeSoto." As these wonderful automobiles are passed on through the generations, their survival is a testimony to their reliability. For many members of the National DeSoto Club, the highlight of the yearly convention is the driving tour. The sight of over 100 DeSotos from all years and models parading through the countryside is enough to make anyone stop and stare. Indeed, after the fifth DeSoto has gone by, factories and houses are emptied as people stand in doorways or on their front lawns to marvel at the beautiful iron roaring down the road. This yearly gathering lines up more DeSotos nose to tail than any other event in the world. The only other time there were so many DeSotos in one place was when they were rolling off the assembly line in Detroit, and that hasn't happened for many decades. At every convention one is sure to hear words like, "Is Wayne bringing his 1930 Roadster?" or "Is Doug bringing his 56 convertible?" Their once-a-year gathering ensures that the torch will be passed on from one generation to the next, and as long as the fire burns, the wonderful DeSoto will never be forgotten.

More great books from Iconografix

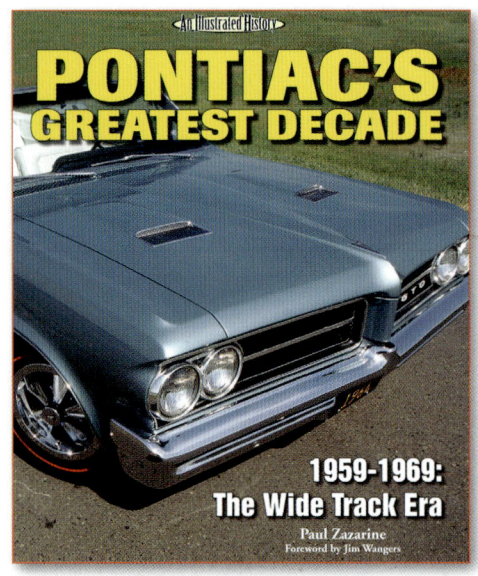

ISBN 1-58388-163-8

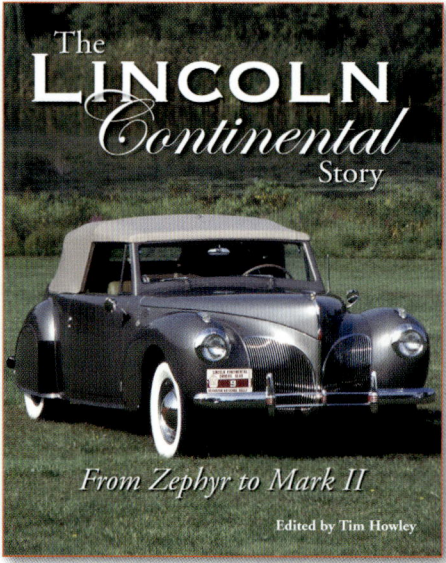

ISBN 1-58388-154-9

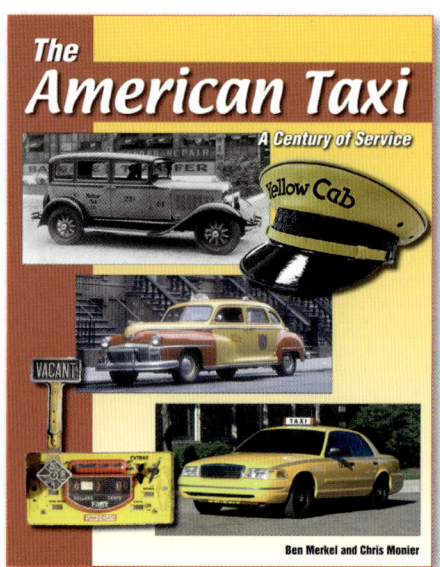

ISBN 1-58388-176-X

ISBN 1-58388-178-6

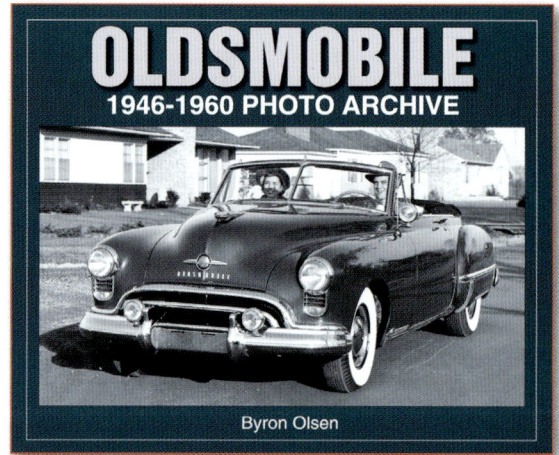

ISBN 1-58388-168-9

ISBN 1-58388-086-0

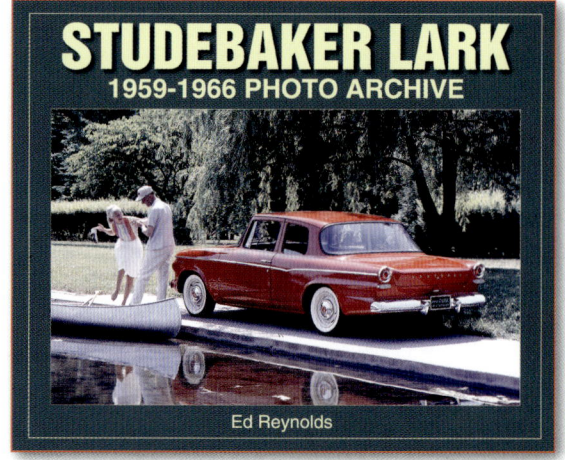

ISBN 1-58388-107-7

Iconografix, Inc. P.O. Box 446, Dept BK, Hudson, WI 54016
For a free catalog call: 1-800-289-3504
info@iconografixinc.com   www.iconografixinc.com